# The Calvinist Universalist

# The Calvinist Universalist

Is Evil a Distortion of Truth? Or Truth Itself?

Stephen Campana

RESOURCE *Publications* · Eugene, Oregon

THE CALVINIST UNIVERSALIST
Is Evil a Distortion of Truth? Or Truth Itself?

Resource Publications
An Imprint of Wipf and Stock Publishers
199 W. 8th Ave., Suite 3
Eugene, OR 97401

www.wipfandstock.com

ISBN 13: 978-1-62564-405-3

Manufactured in the U.S.A.

To all those who refuse to call darkness light, even when it may seem in their best interests to do so. And to my wife, who always believed I could do it—even when I wasn't too sure.

# Contents

# Preface

PRESTON EBY, ONE OF the world's leading Universalists, writes: "If God knew in the beginning that it would turn out like this and included eternal damnation in His creative plans, then why did He create the world in the first place?"[1]

This is not an easy question. Most Christians would be hard-pressed to answer it to their own satisfaction. But a very large body of Christians would have a very easy time answering it. For them eternal damnation does not represent a failure on the part of God; nor was this aspect of His plan an accommodation to events that He did not desire. No, for this group of people eternal damnation was not a crimp in God's plan; it *was* God's plan. He made most of humanity for the very *purpose* of damning them. They are Calvinists. And for the Calvinist eternal damnation is as much a part of God's plan as salvation. Here's how it is expressed in the Presbyterian Confession of Faith:

> "By the decree of God, for the manifestation of his glory, some men and angels are predestinated unto everlasting life, and others foreordained to everlasting death . . . Those of mankind that are predestinated unto life, God, before the foundation of the world was laid, according to his eternal and immutable purpose, and the secret counsel and good pleasure of his will, hath chosen in Christ, unto everlasting glory . . . The rest of mankind, God was pleased . . . to pass by and to ordain them to dishonor and wrath for their sin, to the praise of his glorious justice."[2]

Often Universalist apologists make their case as if Calvinists did not exist. They seem to forget that there exists a large body of people who have a

1. Eby, "Eternity"
2. Thayer, *Theology of Universalism*, 60

ready answer for the question that Eby posed. That is something this book will seek to redress. Let me use another illustration. The author of a Universalist blog pens an essay in which he sets out to

> "reveal a very important Biblical Truth . . . Knowing this truth will automatically lay to rest many myths and misconceptions . . . So what is this Truth? Simply this: *That everything, absolutely everything, always goes according to the will and the plan of God. Always!*"[3]

The author then proceeds to back up his contention with dozens of verses from scripture. He cites verses that establish God's sovereignty over our days:

> "Since [man's] days are determined, the number of his months is with You; You have appointed his limits, so that he cannot pass." (Job 14:5)

He cites verses that establish God's sovereignty over our bodies:

> "Your eyes saw my substance, being yet unformed. And in your book they were all written, the days fashioned for me, when as yet there were none of them." (Psalm 139:16)

He cites verses that establish God's sovereignty over our ways:

> "O LORD, I know the way of man is not in himself; it is not in man who walks to direct his own steps." (Jeremiah 10:23)

And most importantly, he cites verses that establish God's sovereignty over our *wills*.

> "They gathered together to do everything that you, by your power and will, had already decided would take place." (Acts 4:28)

It is this last item—the fact that God exercises strict sovereignty over the human will—that would seem to present an almost Prima facie case for Universalism. And the author of this blog does make a compelling case. There's only one problem: The Calvinist *already* accepts this concept of God's sovereignty. They just believe He *uses* that sovereignty differently. The Calvinist and the Universalist are doing different dances to the same music! Hence, to argue against Calvinism requires a different approach. One must meet them on their own turf. And that means more than simply proving

---

3  Cottington, "The Mother of All Truths."

what they already know. It means proving that they are drawing the *wrong conclusions* from the things they already know. Allow me to illustrate. The Calvinist and the Universalist each employ their own proof text as to why man was created. The Calvinist employs Romans 9:22; the Universalist Romans 8:20.

> Romans 9:22–23: "What if God, willing to show his wrath, and to make his power known, endured with much longsuffering the vessels of wrath fitted to destruction: And that he might make known the riches of his glory on the vessels of mercy, which he had afore prepared unto glory?"

> Romans 8:20–21: "For the creature was made subject to vanity, not willingly, but by reason of him who hath subjected the same, in hope, Because the creature itself also shall be delivered from the bondage of corruption into the glorious liberty of the children of God."

I will now demonstrate that the Calvinist, if he is consistent, must agree with Rom 8:20, while disagreeing with Romans 8:21. The Calvinist believes that in the best of all possible worlds, sin must exist. It must exist because, as Romans 9:22 insists, God must display his glory by punishing it. But if the best of all possible worlds includes sin, then God had to create man not only liable to sin, but *certain* to sin. Hence, he had to "make man subject to vanity." But notice the problem. Romans 8:20 insists that God subjected creation to vanity, not, as the Calvinist insists, to punish him for it, but rather to *free* him from it. Vanity was not created as an end in itself, but as a means to an end. And to this the scriptures agree:

> "Howbeit that was not first which is spiritual, but that which is natural; and afterward that which is spiritual." (1 Cor 15:46)

> "For the Lord will not cast off forever: But though he cause grief, yet he will have compassion according to the multitude of his mercies. For he does not afflict willingly nor grieve the children of men. (Lamentations 3:32–33)

> "It is an experience of evil Elohim [God] has given to the sons of humanity to humble them by it." (Ecclesiastes 3:10)

But Calvinist theology attributes to God an entirely different motive in giving us an "experience of evil"—and an unspeakably fiendish one at that. Calvinist theology, therefore, would require that they render Romans 8:20–21 this way: "For the creature was made subject to vanity, not willingly, but by reason of him who hath subjected the same, in order to torment them forever in hell."

The Calvinist might raise the objection that he does not believe Romans 8:20–21 applies to human beings. No matter. According to his own theology it *does* apply to human beings—at least the first half. His God *had* to make man subject to vanity in order to fulfill His own purposes. We therefore have a verse that perfectly describes the way the Calvinist God *had* to create man, which they say doesn't apply to man because they don't like the next verse!

Notice the flow of my argument. I am only asking the Calvinist to be consistent with his own theological assertions. I am not trying to convince him that a good God doesn't torture people forever because it's *wrong* or that God's total sovereignty over the human will argues against eternal torment because such a thing is *absurd and cruel*. No, I concede from the start that they accept that God, as far as the depraved human mind can see, operates in a way that *is* cruel and absurd. I will, of course, try to prove that they are wrong, but only by showing their own scriptures and their own ideas demand it as a matter of logical consistency.

# PART 1

Is God the Universal Father?

# 1

## A Calvinist's Journey From Eternal Torment to Annihilationism

I did not gain the impression that the theologians who mounted this evasive defense were being willfully dishonest. I think they were sincere. Nevertheless, I was irresistibly reminded of Peter Medawar's comment on Father Teihard de Chardin's *The Phenomenon of Man*, in the course of what is probably the greatest negative review of all time: "its author can be exused of dishonesty only on the grounds that before deceiving others he has taken great pains to deceive himself."

—RICHARD DAWKINS

IF THE NAME HAROLD Camping rings a bell, there's a good reason. He made headlines a while back when he set an exact date for the Rapture. May 21, 2011.[1] That was the day that the Rapture would occur. Absolutely guaranteed. Throngs of his loyal followers devoted themselves to spreading the word. You might recall the billboards proclaiming the news.

Not to spoil the ending, but he was wrong. By how much time will tell. But that's not what's of interest to me here. What's interesting to me is the fact that as Camping's eschatological understanding shifted, so did his understanding of the fate of the wicked. During that time frame he converted from an avid belief in eternal torment to an equally avid belief in Annihilationism. What caused the shift? Simple. He came to understand that the verses depicting the torment of the damned in hell were actually

---

1 Camping, *To God Be The Glory!*, 44.

depicting the torment of being left behind during the Rapture. The verses had absolutely nothing to do with God torturing people forever in a place called hell. A good God, he now declared, would never do such a thing.

Now, here's the interesting part: he did not come to his new position through years of anguished wrestling with the moral implications and logical problems posed by the idea of eternal torment. At least he never said anything to indicate that this was the case. Moreover, anyone familiar with his hermeneutic understood that it did not allow for man to apply his sin-tainted reason and conscience to the scriptures. And by all accounts he retained this hermeneutic during and after his conversion. The fact is that no actual thought went into the conversion at all. He simply came to see that the eternal torment passages could just as easily be describing temporal torment, and on the basis of this discovery, he changed his views. And upon changing his view on what God *would* do to the unsaved, he also changed his views about what God *should* do to the unsaved. Suddenly he realized that eternal torment was a doctrine unworthy of a good God. In fact, it made him "cruel."[2]

But here's the point I want to emphasize: What did this change of heart indicate if not that this is precisely what he had believed all along? I'm not talking about the change in his belief as to the fate of the wicked. I'm talking about the change in his beliefs as to the *fairness* of that fate. Camping used to defend the fairness of hell:

> "The answer to the question of man's accountability to God after the fall is found in the reason for his hopeless condition of slavery to sin and Satan. This frightful condition did not result from a whim or caprice of fate; it did not result from God lashing out in irrational anger for his disobedience. The condition is altogether the result of man's own actions."[3]

But Annihilationist Camping writes: "The traditional view discloses the inherent cruelty and lack of mercy that is part of the nature of unsaved mankind."[4]

Upon discovering that God would not subject people to eternal torment, he also discovered that doing so would be wrong, even after spending decades professing that it was right. Again, this could only mean he had never believed it was right in the first place.

2. Camping, *To God Be The Glory!*, 14.

3. Camping, *God's Magnificent Salvation Plan*, 2.

4. Camping, *To God Be The Glory!*, 14.

## God Hides the Truth

The question, then, is this: What was causing him to profess what he knew deep down was wrong all along? Was there a culprit? Indeed there was, according to Camping. It was God Himself. He had written the bible in such a way that we could not come to truth except in these end times. God had linked "time and judgment" (Ecclesiastes 8:5–6) in such a way that we could not understand the latter without an adequate understanding of the former.

> "Throughout the church age, God has hidden this time information, and an understanding of God's judgment plan, from all mankind, including the churches . . . Because the time information is linked tightly to God's judgment plan, God's judgment plan was also altogether wrongly understood throughout the 1,955 years of the church age . . ."[5]

But is that the real reason Camping could not see that eternal torment was both unbiblical and immoral? It seems to me that Camping's newfound eschatological perspective simply gave him a newfound appreciation of laws that were there all along, with or without a Rapture. He writes:

> "The horrible man-made traditional idea of God's judgment process is a terrible denial of the law of God. The idea was designed with little or no understanding that the entire Bible, which is the Word of God, is therefore, the law of God. Effectively, statements like "the wages of sin is death," and "in the day that thou eatest therefore thou shalt surely die," are looked upon as instructions from the mouth of God, rather than the very law of God".

Here Camping describes the traditional doctrine as a "terrible denial of the law of God," whereas elsewhere, he states:

> Throughout the church age, God has hidden this time information, and an understanding of God's judgment plan, from all mankind, including the churches . . . Because the time information is tightly linked to God's judgment plan, God's judgment plan was also altogether wrongly understood throughout the 1,955 years of the church age . . .

So, which is it? Does the doctrine of eternal torment reflect a denial of God's laws? Or merely the best understanding God Himself made available? Did God really write the bible in such a way that would make us deny His laws and slander His character? Because of *time* issues? What if

5. Ibid 4.

Part 1: **Is God the Universal Father?**

Camping came to the bible insisting on a good God? A loving Father? Is not his failure to do so at least as much to blame for the "terrible" conclusions he reached as the idea that God hid His judgment plan in His "time" plan? To this his own words testify.

> The way each person thinks and believes is a product of the ideas he has accepted to be *true and trustworthy* . . . As additional ideas are presented, they will be filtered and tested in light of the ideas that he has *already accepted* to be true and trustworthy . . . Once we have learned certain religious ideas, and have accepted them as truth, it seems *impossible* to accept any ideas that are not in agreement with the ideas that we have already accepted as truth.

Doesn't Camping read his own words? Clearly the fault was with his hermeneutic, not the timeline factor. And what exactly is his hermeneutic?

> The solution to this problem is: we must go to the bible with no prejudices and no presuppositions whatsoever. If we are to find truth, the presuppositions have to be examined and critiqued as vigorously as any doctrine that we claim to have received from the Bible. We must let the Bible alone guide us into truth. We must recognize that we are human beings with feet of clay; we have sin-tainted minds. Our minds are finite and not like the infinite mind of God. We must hold the position, "let God be true, but every man a liar (Romans 3:4).[6]

But is it really possible to come to the bible with no presuppositions? David Burnfield writes:

> Before starting it is helpful to remind ourselves that how one interprets Scripture has very little to do with one's commitment to the Lord or reverence for His word and everything to do with the theological presuppositions or model one holds to. If one accepts that God will punish people eternally in hell, passages are interpreted one way; if it is believed God will eventually annihilate the wicked, passages are interpreted another way; and if one holds that all will eventually be saved, there is yet a third possibility.
>
> Years before I considered Patristic Universalism, I would think about the difference between exegesis and eisegesis. Exegesis meant you obtained the meaning from the text (a good thing) while eisegesis meant you read the meaning into the text (a bad thing). But for these words (exegesis and eisegesis) to have any meaning, there would have to exist some official, single and

6. Camping, *First Principles of Bible Study*, 12.

authoritative interpretation of each passage of Scripture by which all interpretations could be measured against. But such a standard interpretive canon does not exist so in reality we all commit eisegesis in the minds of anyone who doesn't belong to our particular theological view. [7]

In other words, we all start with presuppositions; the only question is: *Which* presuppositions? Or, as Camping himself puts it:

> The way each person thinks and believes is a product of the ideas he has accepted to be true and trustworthy . . . As additional ideas are presented, they will be filtered and tested in light of the ideas that he has already accepted to be true and trustworthy . . . Once we have learned certain religious ideas, and have accepted them as truth, it seems impossible to accept any ideas that are not in agreement with the ideas that we have already accepted as truth.

And yet Camping insists that the problem was that God hid the truth about judgment in time-line information. But he doesn't really seem to believe it, saying that the traditional doctrine is a "terrible denial of God's laws." As if those laws weren't there all along! Consider what he's saying:

1. Throughout church history, God hid his judgment plan. He allowed the verses of the bible to be constructed in a way that appeared to teach eternal torment.

2. It was a "terrible denial of God's laws" to believe in eternal torment and it reflects the "inherent cruelty and lack of mercy that is part of the nature of unsaved mankind."

But how could it be cruel and terrible to believe what God, as far as we could be expected to see, is actually saying? Camping's own words reveal what he really believes: *Even when the bible seem to paint an evil picture of God, we should not believe them!*

And if he had taken this approach from the start, he would have never preached eternal torment. Regardless of any end time information, or lack thereof. Going "to the Bible with no prejudices and no presuppositions whatsoever" lead him to believe a doctrine that he now calls "cruel." Clearly this indicates that his problem all along was a willingness to give his assent to things that his conscience abhorred. In other words, he was willing to call darkness light when it seemed in his best interests to do so. But even now he cannot see that this was the problem. Why? Because he still clings to the same

7. Burnfield, *Patristic Universalism*, ch 1.

hermeneutic. He still draws his understanding of God's character from the verses rather than interpreting the verses in light of God's revealed character in Christ. His failure to understand this probably accounts for the rather bizarre distinction he makes between himself and everyone else. He does not really seem to think it was morally wrong to preach eternal torment *in his own case.* He was simply disseminating the information God Himself had made available at the time. For *others,* however, it was "cruel." Why the distinction? Apparently, *he* preached eternal torment, not out of cruelty, but out of faithfulness to the revelation available at the time. *Others,* however, were doing it for an entirely different reason. Apparently they came to the bible all too willing to accept an idea that appealed to their fleshly, evil nature. But then why wasn't it just as wrong for him? He never says.

## Acceptable Contradictions and Unacceptable Contradictions

Harold Camping wrote a book called *The Perfect Harmony of the Numbers of the Hebrew Kings.* He wrote it with a very special purpose in mind. He wanted to defend the veracity of the bible against those who believe it contains errors or contradictions of any kind. This was of paramount importance to him. He insisted that there could be no errors or discrepancies of any kind anywhere in the scriptures. All scripture could be harmonized. God wrote the bible in a way so that contradictions would appear only to those who entertained the idea that they were possible in the first place. In fact, God "purposely wrote the Bible to foster unbelief in the hearts of those who do not want the salvation of the Bible. For them, the Bible appears to contain errors, contradictions, and many things that apparently have no relationship to truth."[8] The *Perfect Harmony of the Hebrew Kings* focuses on numbers. Camping wrote a book because he could not tolerate the idea that any of the numbers of the bible could be contradictory. The idea of numerical contradictions in the bible simply could not stand.

Now, let's look at another contradiction. It is one that Camping tolerated in his own mind for 40 years. It is one he endorsed, approved, praised God for, and preached over the radio waves night after night to the whole world. It is this: It is perfectly okay, and indeed even praiseworthy, for God to create men for the purpose of torturing them forever in a place called hell.

Let's think about this for a moment. Let's consider the magnitude of the contradiction involved here. In fact, let's ponder a similar contradiction.

8. Camping, *The Perfect Harmony of the Numbers of the Hebrew Kings,* 10.

Let's ponder the idea that it's okay for a father to conceive a child for the sole purpose of making his life as miserable as he possibly could. Now, imagine for a moment that you are commissioned with the task of convincing the world that this contradiction is in fact true. Moreover, you are given your own media empire, fully staffed, to help you in this endeavor. And you are given ten years to accomplish the task.

Could you do it? Could you convince the world? Could you convince a part of the world? Could you convince even a small minority? Could you convince even a few? Could you convince even *one person*? Could you and your global media empire, broadcasting to the world 24/7 for ten years, in print, radio, television, internet, and movies, convince even *one person* that it was good for a father to conceive a child for the purpose of making him as miserable as possible? Could you even raise enough doubt in anyone's mind to make them at least entertain the possibility? Of course you could not. And what's more, every single conservative Christian in the world would thank God you couldn't! And yet they propose the *very same contradiction* as part and parcel of the gospel they preach.

But of course the Calvinist has heard this argument before and is not impressed. That's because he *does* have an answer to this contradiction. His answer is this: God is not our Father; He is only our Creator! In other words, he answers the contradiction with an *even bigger contradiction*. Thomas Allin put it this way:

> "We are told God is not the Father of all men; He is only their Creator! What a total misapprehension those words imply. What do we mean by paternity and the obligations it brings? The idea rests essentially on the communication of life by the parent to the child. Paternity is for us largely blind and instinctive; but creation is Love acting freely, divinely; knowing all the consequences, assuming all the responsibility involved in the very act of creating a reasonable immortal spirit. It seems, then, very strange to seek to escape the consequences of the lesser obligation, by admitting one still greater; to seek, in a word, to evade the results of a divine universal fatherhood, by pleading that God is only the Creator."[9]

I believe Camping preached eternal torment not, as he believes, because God hid his judgment plan in a complex end-times web, but rather because of his hermeneutic. We cannot come to the bible with *no presuppositions whatsoever* and expect to find truth. Yes, we must come to

---

9. Allin, *Christ Triumphant*, ch 2.

the bible with humility. But we must also come with a certain degree of common sense and courage. We must have the humility to yield up to God those things that we cannot know, the courage to insist on those things we can know, and the wisdom to know the difference.

## Camping the Universalist

So now Camping believes in Annihilation. That is what he now "believes" is the kind of behavior worthy of a benevolent Creator. But is that what he really believes now? Or is it just what he has convinced himself he believes now? Camping has rejected the very *foundation* of eternal torment, which, it must be noted, is the *same* foundation of Annihilationism—God as cruel and merciless—and yet cannot take that extra step towards Universalism. And he can't do it for the same reason he couldn't renounce eternal torment for 40 years. Because *the verses won't allow it.* He's still drawing his understanding of God's character based on his understanding of *the verses* rather than reading the verses in light of God's revealed character.

For many years Family Radio issued a bible tract called *Does God love You?* Basically, the answer was no. This tract did not actually say in so many words that God hated the wicked, but the conclusion was unavoidable. Moreover, Camping did say it on his Open Forum program, citing verses like Psalm 5:5 for support. At that time Camping held to the traditional interpretation of "eternal fire" and other passages indicating eternal torment for the wicked. After becoming an Annihilationist, however, his understanding changed. Camping wrote:

> "Moreover, God in his wonderful kindness gives us an example of eternal fire. When Sodom was destroyed, that fire literally burned, at most, a few days. Yet the fire that destroyed Sodom and Gomorrah is spoken of as "eternal fire." Even as Sodom and Gomorrah, and the cities about them, in like manner giving themselves over to fornication, and going after strange flesh, are set forth for an example, suffering the vengeance of eternal fire." Therefore, we can be assured that for these reasons and other biblical reasons, we can know that the traditional view of eternal damnation is bankrupt . . ."[10]

Along with his new interpretation of "eternal fire" came a new understanding of God's attitude toward men. Camping wrote:

10. Camping, *To God Be The Glory!*, 5.

"There is a mysterious, dynamic personal relationship that exists between God and every person in the human race. This is true not only between God and those whom He has elected to salvation, but it is also true between God and those whom He has not elected, and who, therefore, will most certainly be destroyed. . . . We see it in the fact that by God's law, a murderer must die because he has murdered a human being who was created in the image and likeness of God (Genesis (9:6). We see it in the command that we are to love our enemies. . . . We see it in the warning God gives in Matthew 5:22 that we are not to call anyone "Raca," that is, worthless or fool . . ."[11]

And so we see the progression:

Eternal fire is eternal torment. God is an eternal tormenter. God hates us.

Eternal fire is annihilation. God is an annihilator. God respects us.

First comes the interpretation of verses, then the understanding of God's character. But what if Camping had chosen to believe Ezekiel 16: 53,55, which promises that Sodom, after enduring "eternal fire," will be restored? Well, I suppose if Camping *did* come to believe that, then we would have to add a third phase to the evolution of his beliefs. It would go:

Eternal fire is eternal torment. God is an eternal tormenter. God hates us.

Eternal fire is annihilation. God is an annihilator. God respects us.

Eternal fire is corrective judgment. God is a Father. God loves us.

But what is keeping him from believing the verse in Ezekiel? I suspect it is nothing more than the fact that he doesn't believe any of the verses which declare that God is the Universal Father. If he believed *those* verses, then he would believe the verse in Ezekiel, and he would again change his take on the meaning of "eternal fire" and of his understanding of the purposes and character of God.

In the meantime, however, his unwillingness to consider the possibility of God's total victory leaves him stranded in a no-man's land, mired in theological inconsistencies which he can only resolve with a contrived middle-ground that tries to preserve what's best about God while destroying what's worst.

11. Camping, *I Hope God Will Save Me*, 18–19.

Part 1: **Is God the Universal Father?**

Consider the incoherency of his own current beliefs, which, if he became a Universalist, he would surely recognize. Shortly after converting to Annihilationism, he set out his new-found outlook about judgment in a book called *To God be the Glory*. He wrote:

> "Since we are to love our neighbors as ourselves, we are to truly desire the highest good for them. The highest good is salvation. However, what is the situation if a person dies unsaved? Do we still love him?"[12]

He then goes on to recount the tale of David and Saul, in which David loved Saul to the very end, even though Saul was not saved. Now let's suppose, just for the sake of argument, that Mr. Camping has another eschatological insight that causes him to convert from Annihilationism to Universalism. How would he look at that same story? Surely he would see that his own words contain a contradiction that sticks out like a sore thumb. His argument is this: eternal torment is a terrible doctrine that denies the love of God. We are to love our neighbors; after all, God, doesn't hate anyone. He would never, ever eternally torment Saul, who David loved. He would just annihilate him!

Surely the Universalist Camping would take his argument one step further, maybe to something like this: "God, who loved David, could never hate Saul, and since, as I pointed out in my book, we are to desire salvation for our neighbor, then surely God must, if he loves David, also love Saul and desire his salvation."

What else might Camping the Universalist say? Well, I would venture to guess that when the damns of orthodoxy are broken and the rivers of reason and conscience allowed to flow freely, he might say soemthing like this:

> "*Of course* God, who imprisoned all in unbelief, will have mercy on all."

> "*Of course* God, who killed all in Adam, will make all alive in Christ."

> "*Of course* God, who subjected all to vanity, will set all free."

> "*Of course* God, who condemned all in Adam, will justify them all in Christ."

Otherwise, He is cruel.

---

12. Camping, *To God Be The Glory*, 12.

# 2

## The Hater Creator

I WOULD LIKE TO begin this chapter with a question: Can what divides God and His creatures, who were made in His own image, be bigger than what binds them? Is this possible? The Christian religious system has answered this question with a resounding *Yes*. On this they do not hesitate. They are not as confident when it comes to explaining how such a thing might be possible. Nevertheless, this *is* the answer. Yes, what divides God and His creation is, in the final analysis, bigger than what binds them. Much bigger. And it always will be. And according to the Arminians, there's nothing God can do about it. And according to the Calvinists, there's nothing He *will* do about it.

Which leads me to another question. How did the Christian religious system arrive at such a conclusion? I would like to propose a rather simple answer. It did not start at the beginning. It did not start with God, who is the alpha and the omega. It did not start with His essence, which is love. It did not start with His attitude toward His creation, which is one of jealous ownership. It did not start with His purpose in creation, which is to sum up all things in Christ. It did not start with His purpose in Christ, which is to justify and reconcile all men.

It started with hell. And worked backwards. The following excerpt from an online conversation captures the gist of my meaning.

> "Calvinism does not lead to Universalism, neither does Armin-
> ianism. What leads to UR is combining the two basic principles
> of Calvinism (God is sovereign) and Arminianism (God loves
> all). Ultimately Calvinism and Arminianism reject each other's

founding principle. Arminianism affirms that in regards to man's salvation, man is sovereign, not God. And Calvinism denies that God loves all. And the reason that Arminians affirm man's sovereignty is because their foundational assumption is that some are ultimately not saved and consigned to Hell. And the reason Calvinists dismiss the concept that God loves all is because of their foundational belief that some are ultimately not saved and are consigned to Hell. Both groups have faith in Jesus for the damnation of "others"!

"You're right Andy. The doctrine of Hell is much more foundational to Calvinists and Arminianists than the doctrine of the Atonement. For them the doctrine of the Atonement is built upon the foundation of the doctrine of Hell. Hell is the default condition of man. Take away Hell, and their whole understanding of God, man, and the Atonement is shaken! With Hell being such a foundational subconscious-level worldview assumption, it is difficult for most to even consider that Hell is not true—regardless of how much scriptural evidence there is that counters the doctrine of Hell. So, yes, for them "ETC is the cornerstone of faith, rather than Christ and Him crucified."!!!!

How do we discover God's attitude toward His creatures? There are two ways. We can start with hell and work backward. Or we can start with "God is love" and work forward. The Christian church, historically, has opted for the first method. This most certainly includes the Calvinists, who reason thus:

1. God sends men into the lake of fire

2. The lake of fire is eternal torment

3. Therefore, God is an eternal tormentor

4. Therefore, God is not the father of all men

5. Therefore, being the Creator must entail less obligation than ordinary fatherhood

The problem with this interpretation is that the lake of fire lends itself to a variety of interpretations, and those interpretations depend on *how we understand God as Father.* In other words, the Calvinist believes that number five is true because numbers one through four are true. But number five is true *only if we interpret numbers one through four in light of number five.* Interpret them in light of the idea that God is everyone's father and you come up with a totally different understanding of the lake of fire. How we interpret verses will depend largely on the very fact to be determined—God's attitude toward men; hence the method employed by Calvinists is *circular*.

So, how do we break the circle? We must first determine if God is the Universal Father, and then we must decide if God understands this to imply the obligations normally associated with fatherhood. And we ought not do this by way of an interpretation of verses that do not deal directly with the issue. Instead, we must consult those verses that address the issue directly, for this *does not depend on interpretation*. When we do this, we find many verses insist that God is our father (Ge. 1:27, 9:6; Ps. 82:6; Is. 64:8; Mal. 2:10; Mt. 5:1, 6:9; Mt. 23:1, 9; Ac. 17:22, 28–29; Ep. 3:14–15). Moreover, they link His fatherhood to His role as creator. This dictates—if we are to accept the *traditional Christian hermeneutic* of interpreting the unclear by the clear—that we interpret all bible verses in light of our understanding of fatherhood and the obligations thus entailed. That is because nothing in all the world—or in the bible—is clearer than the meaning and implications of the word father.

Some truths are self-evident and must be used as the *basis* for interpretation. No Calvinist would disagree with these words from the bill of rights: We hold these truths to be self-evident, that all men are created equal. This is clear. It is self-evident. There are almost no words that can describe the weight of evidence needed to overturn this principle. And so unless the bible *explicitly* repudiates this principle, then it stands as the *clear* by which we ought to interpret the *unclear*. The Calvinists do the opposite. Their interpretation of certain verses leads them to conclude that God, by virtue of the fact that He is our creator, is thereby absolved of all responsibility toward us. Fatherhood is canceled out by Creatorhood. This is grotesque logic and perverse hermeneutics.

The bottom line is this: Does God understand the obligations implicit in the act of creation differently than we do? If God does in fact see His role as Creator as something that absolves Him of obligation, than we ought to find this idea expressed somewhere, and its logic explained. This is a matter of no small import, for if this idea—that it's the Creator's right to hate His creation—is true, and is, in a sense, part and parcel of the gospel, then it certainly bears at least some form of exposition. Consider: there were no Calvinists during the time of Christ. Oh, yes, the people of that time had some harsh views of the Almighty, but no Jew of that era preached the kind of things to be found in the works of John Calvin or Jonathan Edwards.

If Christ came to reveal the character of God, then surely we should find something in His words that reflect the sentiments found in the words of these preachers. Something that indicated that God, along with His love for humanity, also harbored a great hatred for this same humanity. It was all the more imperative given the fact that the Jews at that time seemed blissfully unaware of the fact that God had created them for the purpose of torturing them forever in a place called Hell. Hosea Ballou writes:

> "And so there is something also, very unaccountable, if it was believed under the Old and New Testament times, that we never read of any fears having been expressed of a child, or any relative, or friend, or any fellow creature, or anyone, however wicked in this life, having gone to such a place of misery. As it is well observed, by another writer on this subject, who truly says, and it is undeniable that, "If their belief was the same as in our day, why do we never find them express that belief about future eternal punishment, as is now done in books and sermons and in conference meetings, and in common conversation? No man can possibly deny the vast difference between their language, and the common language now used upon the subject. If the language is so different, is it not a presumptive proof that the invention of a new language arose from the unscriptural doctrine that hell was a place of endless misery?
>
> We do not read that they, under the Old or New Testament times, expressed any fears about their children, their relations, their neighbors, or the world at large, going to eternal misery. As to their feelings, I do not find a sigh, nor a tear shed, a groan uttered, a prayer offered, nor any exertions made, as if they believed men were exposed to endless misery in a future state. . . . I find nothing of the kind expressed, either in the way of anticipation before death, or after such persons had been removed from the world . . .
>
> If, in short, this doctrine was then believed, a dead silence, and the most stoical apathy were maintained even by good men, about it."[1]

As this quote makes clear, the idea of an eternal, burning hell did not occupy the same place in ancient Jewish thought as it does in modern Christianity. And most certainly the *concept of the Calvinist God* was absolutely nowhere to be found. The Jews of that era might not have thought that God owed them *love*, but surely the idea that God had conceived them in hatred, and desired only their ruin, and that this was good and noble

1. Ballou, *A Treatise on Atonement*, 207.

of Him, would have come as a great shock to them. And so if this was the message Christ came to bring—a intrinsic part of the *good news*—then surely it would have been referenced in scripture. Surely it deserved the same treatment as other new concepts that Christ brought with Him. For instance, Christ redefines sin to include thoughts and affections. But this new idea is not transmitted via a few cryptic statements whose meaning we must infer; to the contrary the new doctrine is extensively exposited in Romans, along with the nature and purpose of the law. It is not left for us to infer these things; they are stated in a positive form and given the attention they deserve. Take a moment to reflect on that. Christ came announcing *new concepts* of sin. And not only that, but a *new concept* of God. God is *love*. These new concepts are given full treatment in Romans and John, as well as other books of the New Testament.

And so it is only fair to ask: Where is this Calvinist idea of the Creator as Hater given a similar treatment? Where is this new idea—that had never entered the mind of man—given the expected exposition? Surely, Paul, who did not hesitate to bring "the full counsel of God" would have given it at least a chapter or two of his attention. Surely this idea—the most radical in history—would merit some positive consideration. After all, that other radical idea—that God would love us enough to die for us—is treated in great detail. And yet which of the two ideas are more radical? That God, who conferred upon us an unasked for existence, would make provision for us that this existence might turn out to be a good thing? Or that God would create us for no other reason than to make us as miserable as possible forever and ever? If we are honest, we must admit that the second idea is far more incomprehensible. And so we would expect that if it were true, then it would be explained in the gospel record, for is not the good of the gospel—man's salvation—to be understood against the backdrop of the bad—his sin and what he's being saved from? Is it possible that the *rationale* for this backdrop—the fact that God hates us—should receive no mention?

Romans 11:22 says "behold the goodness and severity of God." Throughout the bible God's severity is always pictured as a corollary of His love. It is never presented as something which flows from a disposition of hatred. We read only that God is love, not that He is hatred. That He died for every man, not that He reprobated most men who ever lived. That He desires that none perish, not that He desires that most perish. There's never a word about being saved from a God who hates us. If God conceives us in hate, then the curse man is under is not death; it's *life*. But the bible never suggests this horrific thing. The enemy is death. That's how it's always presented. If Calvinism is true, we were cursed in the counsels of eternity past, long before death entered the scene. It has nothing to do with death, and everything to do with life. The curse was not death at all—death would be a *blessing*. The curse was life. Existence itself was the curse. The bible, however, represents the enemy as sin, and death as the result. But if Calvinism is true, then *God* is the enemy and death is the result of *life*. This is not consistent with the biblical witness. Death is something that reflects a rift between man and God; it's not a symptom, or evidence, of a *pre-existing* rift that is rooted in God's own natural disposition toward us. Adam—*mankind*—is pronounced very *good*, not very *hated*, before sin and death get in the way.

The fact is that the whole notion is something that must be assumed and then read back into the scriptures. The reason for the assumption, of course, is that not all men are saved in this lifetime. If they're not saved, the thinking goes, then God hates them. Why else would He allow them to perish? Doesn't this fact demand the inference that the Calvinists have devised? After all, isn't it strange that God would allow some men to die unsaved unless He did so for the purpose of eternally damning them?

Actually, there's nothing strange about it. I believe the idea that God would save all men in this lifetime is actually much stranger. Imagine a world in which every man who ever lives at some point in their life confess Christ as Lord. Consider what such a thing would involve. First, every one who is conceived actually has to be born. No still-births, no abortions, no miscarriages. Secondly, everyone has to hear the gospel. This means there could exist no pagan nations. This means no Buddhism, no Hinduism, no Islam, no Taoism, etc. . . . As every man is a Christian, so every nation is a Christian nation. Thirdly, it means that every one who is born into the world is privileged to possess a sound mind—at least sound enough to understand the gospel when they hear it. And fourthly, it means that Christ's ministry would have had to occur, not thousands of years after Adam, but during Adam's lifetime. The necessity for this is obvious. Millions died between Adam and Christ without ever hearing the gospel. This could not be permitted if all must hear and confess during their own lifetimes. The first Adam, therefore, could not pre-date the second Adam. Their work of sin and salvation, respectively, had to occur simultaneously. Christ had to shadow Adam. Even as the first man was eating the apple, the second had to be hanging on the cross. Is that what God had in mind when He inspired

Paul to write: "Howbeit that was not first which is spiritual, but that which is natural; and afterward that which is spiritual" (1 Cor. 15:46)?

Does anybody really believe that when God told Adam "the wages of sin is death" that He had *that* in mind? A tidy process that unfolds with clockwork regularity and precision? *That's* the vanity to which the creation would be subjected (Rom 8:20)? No, it seems evident that when God issued His warning, He planned that death would run its full course over all of creation. Only then could we appreciate how truly awful it is. We had to see it in all of its horror. We had to see all of the things that give death its sting, the things that distinguish it from life. We had to see its suddenness, as it strikes without warning, ripping people from there loved ones in an instant. We had to see its randomness, as it claims children and babies and infants. We had to see its relentlessness, as it stalks its victims, slowly and methodically, like a boxer cutting off the ring, closing in inch by inch, before finally lowering the boom. In almost all of its motions, death shows its ugly face. We see it strike too fast, leaving loved ones with no chance to say goodbye. We see it move too slow, leaving its victims and their families praying for the end. And even in those rare instances when death is kind, allowing its victim to live a long life before taking him peacefully in his sleep, it still shows its capriciousness, for one is left to ask: Why do some get to go out so easy, while others must suffer so much?

But none of this could have happened had God decided to save all men in their lifetime. Indeed such a plan would require that God practically remove from death the one feature that most distinguishes it from life—its *chaos*. The very idea is absurd. *Of course* God did not have such a plan in mind when He subjected the creation to vanity. If He wished to devise a plan that would proceed with regularity and clockwork precision, free from all randomness and chaos, and almost totally devoid of the sting of death, then He could have devised no greater plan than to *keep Adam from sinning in the first place!* What kind of atrophied imagination leads people to believe that the only possible reason God might have for letting men perish is to torture them forever in a place called Hell?

*Of course* it is not God's will that every man comes to Christ during his lifetime. God has a time table. Each man is to be saved "in his own order" (1 Cor 15:23). In the meantime, we perish. Does that mean we are lost forever? No. The bible records many instances of eternal punishment that were not eternal (Deut. 23:3,6; Ezra 10:2,3,44; Neh. 13:1, 23, 25, 30; Jer. 48:42; Ezek. 21:28, 32;Jer. 48:47, 49:6; Isa. 19:21, 25; Jude 1:7, Ezek. 16:53,

55). It also makes it perfectly clear that many who could have very easily been saved were not, and the implication is obvious that they are to be a part of a universal judgment that will one day result in the salvation of all (Mt. 11:21; Phil. 2:10).

Which brings me back to my main point. Men perish because God saves on his own time-table, not because He hates them. If He hated them, then Christ would have revealed this fact. Not only did He not reveal it; He said just the opposite. And so, having disposed of the idea that God *must* hate us because some perish, we come back to our original point. If God hates us, where is the evidence from scripture? Again, the people of that time had no conception of the Calvinist Hater Creator. If this is truly what God is like, then surely the bible must tell us so. Does it? Do we find the expected exposition? Is it anywhere even hinted at? It is not. But do we at least find God *distancing* Himself from His creatures and from the traditional understanding of fatherhood? Even the Christian religious system is smart enough to do this. They try to place a certain *distance* between man and God by suggesting that God made us not out of Himself—an idea that would seem to suggest an indivisible link—but out of *nothing*, as if such a thing actually exists, or as if the distinction even matters (doesn't nothing come from God, too)? But does God distance Himself from this idea? Let's see. We read in Acts 17:26–28:

> "And has made of one blood all nations of men for to dwell on all the face of the earth, and hath determined the times appointed, and the bounds of their habitation; That they should seek the Lord, if haply they might feel after Him, and find Him, though He be not far from every one of us: For in Him we live, and move, and have our being; as certain also of your own poets have said, For we are also His offspring."

What a strange thing for the Calvinist God to say! Perhaps it was an abberation. Is the principal anywhere repeated?

> You are our Father . . . our potter; and all we are the work of Your hand (Is. 64:8).

> For of him, and through him, and to him, are all things . . . (Rom. 11:36)

And perhaps most importantly of all,

> Have we not all one Father? Has not one God created us? (Mal. 2:10)

7. He justifies every man (Rom. 5:18) "Therefore as by the offense of one judgment came upon all men to condemnation; even so by the righteousness of one the free gift came upon all men unto justification of life."

8. He desires that all men be saved (1 Tim. 2:3–5) "For this is good and acceptable in the sight of God our Saviour; who will have all men to be saved, and to come unto the knowledge of the truth."

9. He has every tongue confess Christ as Lord (Philippians 2:10) "That at the name of Jesus every knee should bow, of things in heaven, and things in earth, and things under the earth; and that every tongue should confess that Jesus Christ is Lord, to the glory of God the Father."

Now, let's pause for a moment to consider what I have just done and, just as importantly, what I have not done. First, I employed a bible translation that is known to be favorably disposed toward the opposing viewpoint. Then, using that translation, I gathered nine verses of scripture that comprised nine essential points in the meta-narrative of the gospel. Each of these points bears a tight link, both logically and biblically, to the one that precedes it. Each one builds on the one before it and flows logically—one might say inescapably—from it. In building this chain at no point did I embellish any verses. In no way did I ever deviate from the historical grammatical method. I never suggested one word did not carry its ordinary meaning. I never asked that the natural meaning of the words employed be interpreted in light of a *less* clear verse of scripture; nor did I engage in any *eisegesis*. And yet, merely by taking these verses, drawn from an unfavorable translation, and arranging them in logical sequence, I was able to demonstrate what would appear to be a clear plan by God to save all men. And more importantly to the subject at hand, I was able to demonstrate that He *loves* all men. This the Calvinist denies with a passion. And so I ask: how might they answer this scripture chain? Could they rebuff these nine points—either as a unit or individually—while employing the same biblically sound methods that I did? Let's see how they might answer each of the nine points I laid out.

1. God is love (1 Jn. 4:8)

Most likely they would concede this point, but they would add that He is also a consuming fire. Is this a valid answer to this verse and the implications it entails? I don't see how it is. By consuming fire, the Calvinist means that God is an eternal tormentor. It is impossible to see how He can be both love and an eternal tormentor. Of course this doesn't mean that the Calvinist cannot find some circuitous way around this problem; they can, of course. But remember what I accomplished in these nine points. I made each point without engaging in any eisegesis. I simply presented the verses *as they are* in the King James version of the bible. I provided no commentary; I let the verses stand on the own merit. Can the Calvinist do this with regards to the verse "God is love"? Of course not. He must *explain* what God is love *really* means. And the explanation will insist that ultimately we reject understanding this verse by the historical grammatical method whereby words retain their ordinary meaning.

Do I have to do the same thing with regard to the verse "God is a consuming fire" in order to reconcile it with "God is love"? Not at all. Purifying fire is an essential part of love. Fire can *serve* love; hence the two are a perfect match. But how can fire—when understood as eternal torment—possibly serve love? And so my beginning point—the essence of God—for the meta-narrative of the gospel is set forth easily and without any need for violating sound biblical principles of interpretation. The Calvinist cannot say the same. And so I would be well within my rights to conclude the matter right here, for the simple fact is that the Calvinist has no basis to even begin building his case. He cannot reconcile His own concept of God's essence without violating the proper rules of interpretation.

2. He made man in His own image (Gen. 1:27) "So God created man in his own image, in the image of God he created him; male and female he created them."

What do the Calvinists do with this verse? Now, remember the Calvinist says God made us to *hate* us. Then why does He create us—*all* of us—in His *own* image and then declare us *very good*? How can such a thing possibly be understood without ignoring all three of the biblical methods of interpretation they profess to follow? By what *normal* understanding does the idea of creating in one's own image entail *hating* that creature? How is it even permitted according to *sound rules of biblical interpretation*?

Perhaps at this point the Calvinist might appeal to the Perfect Adam theory. God did not hate Adam at the start; the hatred came in after the fall. There are more things wrong with this assertion than can be treated in a thousand books; hence I will confine myself to two. First off, the Calvinists trace God's hatred to an eternal decree that pre-dates the fall, and was not contingent upon it; therefore God did in fact hate us even at our creation, at which time He made us in His *own image* and declared us *very good*. This is surely a position which one cannot defend without violating our three rules of bible interpretation. Secondly, the entire Perfect Adam theory is quite literally *based* on interpreting the clear by the unclear.

> The clear: "It is sown in corruption; it is raised in incorruption: It is sown in dishonour; it is raised in glory: it is sown in weakness: it is raised in power . . ." (1 Cor 15:42–43)

> The unclear: You are the anointed cherub that covers; and I have set you so; you were upon the holy mountain of God; you have walked up and down in the midst of the stones of fire. You were perfect in your ways from the day that you were created, till iniquity was found in you . . ." (Ezekiel 28:14–15)

3. He creates them for His pleasure (Rev. 4:11) ". . . for thou hast created all things, and for thy pleasure they are and were created."

The Calvinist believes God will derive pleasure from torturing people in hell forever. But is that the *normal* understanding of a verse like Rev. 4:11? Or of a verse like Col. 1:15–17: "Who is the image of the invisible God, the firstborn of every creature: For by him were all things created . . . all things were created by him and *for* him: And he is before all things, and by him all things consist"?

The Calvinist would have us believe this verse is saying something like this: "All things were created by him and for him, that he might derive pleasure by torturing most of them in hell forever." But these verses carry no such implication. Such a meaning is unthinkable according to any method whereby words retain their ordinary meaning and implications. The "pleasure" spoken of is linked to the act of creation, and the normal implications—the *good will*—implied in such an act is not denied, but *affirmed* by these verses. Likewise, in Acts 17:26–28 we read:

> "And has made of one blood all nations of men for to dwell on all the face of the earth, and hath determined the times appointed, and the bounds of their habitation; That they should seek the Lord, if haply they might feel after Him, and find Him, though He be not far from every one of us: For in Him we live, and move, and have our being; as certain also of your own poets have said, For we are also *His offspring*."

The Calvinist, when confronted by verses that seem to imply that God desires that all men be saved, appeal to the idea that God has a revealed will and a hidden will. His revealed will is to save all men; His hidden will is to damn most. Okay, let's grant the premise. Let's suppose God does have a hidden will which the Calvinists have managed to uncover. If God is in fact hiding His will, we would at the very least expect Him to do so with some consistency. We would expect Him to take a particular posture—one of detached benevolence, perhaps—and stick to it. But does He? It would seem that He can't make up His mind. In Ezekiel 33:11 He explicitly—and by way of a *swear* no less—*denies* taking pleasure in the death of the wicked. In Romans 9:22, according to Calvinists, He explicitly *affirms* taking such pleasure. But what in God's name is He doing in Col. 1:15–20 and Rev. 4:11? Is He denying or affirming? Is He hiding, as in Ezek. 33:11, or revealing, as in Rom. 9:22? In Rev. 4:11 we see the exact same "all things" referenced in Phil. 2:10, which undoubtedly refers to all men who have ever lived, engaged in the act of *praising* Christ. If God is *revealing* the truth here, then presumably we are to read the verse this way: " . . . for thou hast created all things, and for thy pleasure they are and were created, the pleasure of saving some, and the pleasure of torturing some in hell forever." This is how God *reveals* that He takes pleasure in tormenting His creatures? By showing them all surrounding His throne in *worship*? Obviously, the answer must be that He is hiding. He must be hiding the fact that He derives pleasure from torturing His creatures by explicitly affirming the exact opposite!

And how to take Acts 17:26–28? Obviously, God is *hiding* again. But how exactly is He hiding anything in these words? He is drawing the tightest possible link between the act of creation and the good will thus implied. There is simply no other context in which to take these words. This verse goes far beyond detached benevolence; this verse, if the Calvinism is true, can only be understood as an outright lie. And so we are confronted with the inexplicable fact that if God is hiding the truth, then He is doing so by way of a rather cumbersome method whereby sometimes He hides, sometimes He reveals, and sometimes, if words have any meaning at all, He lies.

But I digress. What about the verses Calvinists use to show that God did in fact create us to hate us? What about Proverbs 16:4? "The LORD hath made all things for himself: yea, even the wicked for the day of evil." The following explanation for this verse was offered by a website that believes in eternal torment:

> In the above passage, the phrase, "things for Himself" takes us
> back to the Hebrew word maaneh, which is to answer to, or to give
> a reply to. What is being said in the first part of this verse is, "The

Lord hath made all things to answer or give an account unto Him." With that said, we could accurately read Proverbs 16:4 like this:

*The LORD hath made all things to give account unto Him: yea, even the wicked, who think they are off His hook, have to give an account unto Him on the day of judgment.*

Doesn't that make a lot more sense? Now let's put that verse into context with verses 2 through 5:

16:2 All the ways of a man are clean in his own eyes; but the LORD weigheth the spirits.

16:3 Commit thy works unto the LORD, and thy thoughts shall be established.

16:4 [The LORD hath made all things to give account unto Him: yea, even the wicked, who think they are off His hook, have to give an account unto Him on the day of judgment.]

16:5 Every one that is proud in heart is an abomination to the LORD: though hand join in hand, he shall not be unpunished.[2]

The bottom line is this: There are no verses in the bible that *explicitly* say that God derives pleasure from tormenting anyone, and several that explicitly say He *doesn't* (Ezek. 33:11, 2 Peter 3:9, Lam. 3:32). The Calvinists can only defend their position by interpreting the clear verses that say He does not rejoice in our suffering with the unclear verses that suggest He does.

4. He claims ownership of man.

Does God view ownership as something that entails no obligations? The following two verses alone would seem to provide a clear answer.

"Behold all souls are mine." (Ezek. 18:4)

"If any provide not for his own, and specially for those of his own house, he hath denied the faith and is worse than an infidel." (1 Tim. 5:8)

How could the Calvinist possibly fit these two verses—and the message entailed—into their theological system except by blatantly violating sound principles of bible interpretation?

5. He is the father of all men (Malachi 2:10) "Have we not all one father? Hath not one God created us?"

---

2. Did God make the wicked for punishment? (Author name not given).

## Part 1: Is God the Universal Father?

The Calvinists like to say God is not our Father; He is only our Creator. In other words, they seek to avoid a logical paradox—the idea of a father who enjoys tormenting his children—by proposing a *bigger* paradox—a *Creator* who enjoys tormenting his creatures. Thomas Allin put it this way:

> "We are told God is not the Father of all men; He is only their Creator! What a total misapprehension those words imply. What do we mean by paternity and the obligations it brings? The idea rests essentially on the communication of life by the parent to the child. Paternity is for us largely blind and instinctive; but creation is Love acting freely, divinely; knowing all the consequences, assuming all the responsibility involved in the very act of creating a reasonable immortal spirit. It seems, then, very strange to seek to escape the consequences of the lesser obligation, by admitting one still greater; to seek, in a word, to evade the results of a divine universal fatherhood, by pleading that God is only the Creator."[3]

But what about verses that imply God is not the Universal Father, like John 8:37–45? There is nothing in those verses whereby God renounces the fatherhood that is necessarily implied in the act of creation. Regarding this issue, Thomas Thayer writes:

> It may be thought that John 8:37–45, requires some notice, since here Jesus not only seems to deny that God was the Father of the unbelieving Jews, but expressly declares the devil to be their father. But he is speaking in this case simply of moral resemblance, or likeness in character. They were children of the devil, or the devil was their father, because they were alike in character. The devil was "a murderer from the beginning," and "ye seek to kill me;" "he is a liar, and the father of it," and ye choose a lie, for "I tell you the truth, and ye believe me not;" and thus "ye are of your father the devil." As they were in moral character or resemblance the children of the devil, so they could not, *in this respect*, claim God as their Father, for there was no likeness between them. Verses 39, 40 explain the meaning:—"If ye were Abraham's children, ye would do the works of Abraham;" just as he says, verse 42, "If God were your Father, ye would love me." Of course they *were* Abraham's children by nature or descent; but they were not morally, because *Abraham* was distinguished for his faith, and they for their unbelief."[4]

---

3. Allin, *Christ Triumphant*, 6.
4. Thayer, *Theology of Universalism*, 90.

Moreover, Malachi 2:10 and Isa. 64:8 clearly tie in God's role as Father to his role as Creator. He is our father because he *created* us and there is *nothing* that can ever change that. How can we try to harmonize scripture when we *begin* by discarding the plain meaning of this word, or, worse yet, declare that it is cancelled out by the fact that the father in question is also the Creator?

6. He had Christ taste death for all men (Heb. 2:9) "But we see Jesus . . . that by the grace of God should taste death for every man."

The Calvinist, of course, would deny that this verse means what it says. And this is precisely my point. It is not the supposedly *unbiblical* Universalist who must deny what this verse *actually* says; it is the Calvinist.

7. He justifies every man (Rom. 5:18) "Therefore as by the offense of one judgment came upon all men to condemnation; even so by the righteousness of one the free gift came upon all men unto justification of life."

One can only deny the obvious scope and intent of these verses by denying that which is right before their eyes. And this cannot be done by using sound principles of biblical interpretation.

8. He desires that all men be saved (1 Tim. 2:3–5) "For this is good and acceptable in the sight of God our Saviour; who will have all men to be saved, and to come unto the knowledge of the truth."

How does the Calvinist explain this verse? By saying God desires all *kinds* of men to be saved, not literally all men. But notice that once again they must deny what the verse actually *says* in favor of what they *think* it says. But then how do they explain Ezek. 33:11?

> ". . . 'As I live,' says the Lord God, 'I have no pleasure in the death of the wicked, but that the wicked turn from his way and live.'"

Does wicked here denote only the saints? Those who are wicked at one point, but then repent? I doubt that even many Calvinists would go that far. No, the fact is that if God does desire that the wicked perish, then He has taken heroic measures to hide this desire. But why did God not see fit to stress in the bible the very fact the Calvinists do in their sermons? Why do they take such perverse pleasure in defending a desire on God's part that He Himself never saw fit to express? One writer put it this way:

> "In short, I cannot see the propriety of saying that God *will* have *all* men to be saved, and to come unto the knowledge of the truth, if he predestinated, from all eternity, millions for endless misery; and if he created any to glorify him, in endless torments, I cannot

see why he should not be willing for them to perish, and answer the end for which he made them."[5]

9. Every tongue confesses Christ as Lord (Philippians 2:10) "That at the name of Jesus every knee should bow, of things in heaven, and things in earth, and things under the earth; and that every tongue should confess that Jesus Christ is Lord, to the glory of God the Father."

How one interprets this—and like verses—will, needless to say, depend on how they interpret the other eight verses, and the implications entailed; hence I will not bother the reader with a detailed argument as to why this verse should mean what it seems to be saying. Sufficient to the point at hand is that it does *seem* to be saying, by normal understanding, precisely what the Calvinists insist it's *not* saying.

And so this completes our journey through the meta-narrative of the gospel story, and as we see, the Calvinist cannot rebut it without consistently and violently violating all of the rules of sound biblical interpretation which they profess to practice. They must challenge the meta-narrative of the gospel at every single point. Is this not extraordinary? Is it not presumptive proof that there is something lacking in their understanding? Simply consider all of the corrections to scripture the Calvinists must make.

- When the bible says God is love, they say: But what that really means is . . .

- When the bible says He created man in His own image, they say: Yes, but this means *absolutely nothing.*

- When the bible says He created man for His own pleasure, they say: Yes, but it's His *pleasure* to torture them forever in hell.

- When the bible says He has claimed ownership of man, they say: Yes, but only in order to *give them over to the devil forever*!

- When the bible says He is the father of all men, they say: He's not our father; He's only our creator!

- When the bible says Christ tasted death for every man, they say: Oh, no He didn't!

- When the bible says He justified every man, they say: Not true!

- When the bible says He desires that all men be saved, they say: Wrong; He desires that most be damned!

5. Ballou, *A Treatise on Atonement*, 188.

- When the bible says that every tongue will confess Christ as Lord, they say: Yes, but only because they are forced to do it!

And most incredibly of all, the Calvinists do all of this in the name of *context*. The Universalist is reading these verses out of *context*. And exactly what context are we taking them *out of*? Simple. We are taking them out the context of *hell*.

# 3

## God's Hidden Will

HOPEFULLY, THE LAST CHAPTER helped to clarify exactly where Calvinism and Universalism part ways. I believe it is impossible to overestimate the importance of this fact. We are looking at nothing less than two separate and distinct ways of understanding God's attitude toward men. Calvinism draws this understanding based on its interpretation of verses that appear to teach that men are eternally damned. Universalism draws its understanding based on verses that specifically address God's attitude toward men. Calvinism reasons this way:

- God sends men into the lake of fire
- The lake of fire is eternal torment
- Therefore, God is an eternal tormentor
- Therefore, God is not the father of all men
- Therefore, being the Creator must entail less obligation than ordinary fatherhood

  Universalism reasons this way:

- God is love
- The lake of fire is God's corrective discipline

  Universalism starts with a rigid understanding of *God is love* and a narrow understanding of the implications this implies. Accordingly, it interprets the lake of fire in light of this fact. The lake of fire, therefore, is God's purifying fire. It is a symbol, to be interpreted as such. But not so with *God is love* and the obligations entailed in creation. They are non-negotiable, the clear by which we must interpret the unclear. Calvinism, on the other hand, takes the lake of fire to mean eternal torment, and interprets God's love accordingly. For Calvinism, the lake of fire is the clear by which by which we must interpret the unclear.

So, which way makes more sense? Either way God is hiding something from someone. This, of course, is in agreement with Calvinism, which states that God has both a hidden will and a revealed will. And so we are presented with two possibilities: Either God is hiding His plan to save all men, or, He is hiding His plan to damn most men.

Let's look at both possibilities. First, let's suppose that God is hiding His plan to save all men. Now, what would that involve? Specifically, how is He hiding this plan? Well, mostly by the use of imagery and symbols, like the lake of fire. This is a fitting way to hide things, and, of no small consequence, the way the bible itself would seem to indicate that God hides things, for the bible says no scripture is its own interpretation; we are to compare spiritual with spiritual in order to search out the meaning of anything which, on the face of it, may be unclear (1 Cor. 2:13). And so on the Universalist model God, who is love, and creates us in His image, and declares us very good, and claims jealous ownership of us, and desires all be saved, and tastes death for all of us, and justifies all of us, is hiding His plan to save all men by the use of symbolic language.

Now, let us suppose God is hiding His plan to *damn* most of humanity. How is He hiding it? Via symbols, as in the first scenario? Well, no. If He is hiding it, then He is doing so by other methods. Three to be exact.

1. By employing plain statements that do not mean what they say

2. By making logical links which cannot be understood by sound biblical interpretation to mean anything other than a plan to save all men

3. By making our senses mediums of deception and assuring that all of our knowledge serves no other purpose than to make us more stupid

Let's take them in order.


## Plain Statements of Scripture

- Therefore as by the offense of one judgment came upon all men to condemnation; even so by the righteousness of one the free gift came upon all men unto justification of life. (Romans 5:18)

- As in Adam all die, so in Christ shall all be made alive. (1 Cor. 15:22)

- He has concluded all in unbelief that he might have mercy on all. (Rom. 11:36)

- For the creation was subjected to futility, not willingly, but because of Him who subjected it, in hope; because the creation itself also will be delivered from the bondage of corruption into the glorious liberty of the children of God. (Rom. 8:20)

- He is the image of the invisible God, the firstborn over all creation. For by Him all things were created that are in heaven and that are on earth, visible and invisible. . . . All things were created through Him and for Him. And He is before all things, and in Him all things consist. . . . For it pleased the Father that in Him all the fullness should dwell, and by Him to reconcile all things to Himself, by Him, whether things on earth or things in heaven, having made peace through the blood of His cross. (Col. 1:15–20)

- That in the dispensation of the fullness of times he might gather together in one all things in Christ, both which are in heaven, and which are in earth . . . (Ephesians 1:10–11)

- Who will have all men to be saved, and to come unto the knowledge of the truth (1 Tim. 2:5)

- For therefore we both labour and suffer reproach, because we trust in the living God, who is the Savior of all men, especially of those that believe. (1 Tim. 4:10)

- And I, if I be lifted up, will draw all men unto me. (Jn. 12:32)

- That at the name of Jesus every knee should bow, of those in heaven, and of those on earth, and of those under the earth, and that every tongue should confess that Jesus Christ is Lord, to the glory of God the Father. (Phil. 2:10–11)

## Presenting deceptive logical links

Earlier we looked at the following facts from scripture:

- God is love (1 Jn. 4:8)

- He creates man in His own image (Gen. 1:27) "So God created man in his own image, in the image of God he created him; male and female he created them."

- He creates them for His pleasure (Rev. 4:11) ". . . for thou hast created all things, and for thy pleasure they are and were created."

- He claims ownership of man (Ezek. 18:4) "Behold all souls are mine."

- He is the father of all men (Malachi 2:10) "Have we not all one father? Hath not one God created us?"

- He had Christ taste death for all men (Heb. 2:9) "But we see Jesus . . . that by the grace of God should taste death for every man."

- He justifies every man (Rom. 5:18) "Therefore as by the offense of one judgment came upon all men to condemnation; even so by the righteousness of one the free gift came upon all men unto justification of life."

- He desires that all men be saved (1 Tim. 2:3–5) "For this is good and acceptable in the sight of God our Saviour; who will have all men to be saved, and to come unto the knowledge of the truth."

- He has every tongue confess Christ as Lord (Philippians 2:10) "That at the name of Jesus every knee should bow, of things in heaven, and things in earth, and things under the earth; and that every tongue should confess that Jesus Christ is Lord, to the glory of God the Father."

We are looking at more than simply verses here. We are looking at inescapable logical links between concepts which are embodied in these verses. We have already proven that the Calvinists can only escape these links by blatantly violating their own rules for sound biblical interpretation.

## Making Our Senses Mediums of Deception

Let us now consider the truly heroic lengths to which God has gone in order to hide the so-called truth of Calvinism. He has not only inspired holy men of old to issue many statements which, when taken in their ordinary sense, would imply universal salvation, but He has also done two other things: First, He has inextricably woven in His word the act of creation with the good will thus implied, and He has *explicitly* equated this act with *fatherhood* (Malachi 2:10, Is. 64:8, Acts 17:26–28, Col. 1:15–17). Secondly, He has planted deep within the heart of every man a sense that a father ought to be *good* to His children rather than evil. And so we see that it is very deceptive and very wicked of the Calvinists to say that God is merely hiding truth through His word. No, He is going much further than that. He is hiding it by making all of our senses into nothing more than mediums of deception and by making all of our knowledge serve no other purpose than to make us more stupid.[1] And He has employed scripture, not to dispel of us this illusion, but to reinforce it. And so the choice between Universalism and Calvinism boils down to two options. Either:

> God is hiding, through the use of a symbol in His word, His plan to save all men.

Or,

> He is hiding His plan to damn most men by *making all of our senses deceive us and then reinforcing that deception with testimony from the bible.*

Now, the bible is clear: God hides the truth to make the wise look stupid (Mt. 11:24, 1 Cor. 1:20–27, 3:19). But how can someone look stupid for believing what God has gone to such heroic lengths to make them believe? By contrast, suppose the Calvinist, on judgment day, finds out that he was wrong. How foolish will he feel to know that he jettisoned every ounce of reason and conscience, disregarded plain statements of scripture, explained away logically unavoidable links, and reasoned that "God is not our father; He's only our creator" simply because of his wrong interpretation of a symbol?

And finally, if the Calvinists are right, and God is hiding His glorious damnation plan, then one cannot hep but wonder: Who is He hiding it *from*? Practically the whole Christian world has figured it out. They may not all believe God *wants* to damn people, but they all believe He *will*. And so, in the final analysis, we are left with the curious fact that, if Calvinism is true, then God has taken enormous pains to hide His will from all but a few, but has failed to do even that!

---

1. Ballou, *Treatise on Atonement* 77.

# 4

## A Matter of Principle

IN THE LAST CHAPTER I endeavored to demonstrate that the Calvinist can only defend the principles that comprise his theological system by violating the rules of biblical interpretation that he claims to follow. Specifically, I set forth a cherished Calvinist premise—God's separateness from His creation—which, if true, ought to be found everywhere in scripture, and showed that not only is it not found, but that in its place we find its opposite. I will now continue this theme by setting forth ten principles which, if eternal torment is true, ought to be denied, and yet are not denied, but very strongly affirmed. You will note that I said these principles are not consistent with eternal torment, not that they are inconsistent with Calvinism. That's because some principles which are quite inconsistent with eternal torment are also part and parcel of Calvinism. Nevertheless, I believe that all of these principles in some measure do argue against Calvinism; hence I have included them all in the same heading. In keeping with the theme of this chapter, I shall also argue that the implications of these principles can only be denied by violating our three methods of sound biblical interpretation. These principles are as follows:

1. We act according to our natures

2. We do not have free will

3. God is mindful of our frame

4. God is our father

5. God created man in His own image

6. It is possible to lie for God

7. God sees the act of creation as suggesting a bond

8. God sees a link between subjecting us to vanity and releasing us from it

9. Sin against man is sin against God

10. There's no such thing as disinterested benevolence

## 1. We Act According to Our Nature

> Matthew 12:33: "Either make the tree good, and his fruit good; or else make the tree corrupt, and his fruit corrupt: for the tree is known by its fruit."
>
> 1 Cor 15:42 "It is sown in corruption; it is raised in incorruption: It is sown in dishonour; it is raised in glory: it is sown in weakness: it is raised in power . . ."
>
> Romans 8:20: "The creature was made subject to vanity . . ."

The simple fact, to which reason attests beyond all question, is that we act according to our natures. In its zeal to defend eternal torment, the Christian religious system has, to a very large extent, denied this simple truth. And this applies to Calvinists as well, most of whom make at least some form of appeal to the Perfect Adam theory in order to justify their doctrine. Consider how five point Calvinist Harold Camping justifies his Calvinistic views:

> "The answer to the question of man's continued accountability to God after the fall is found in the reason for his hopeless condition of slavery to sin and Satan. . . . The condition is altogether the result of man's own actions. God created man good, with every conceivable blessing; and because he was created in the image of God, he was fully responsible for the consequences of his disobedience . . ."[1]

But oddly enough, the bible not only never suggests that it may be possible for a perfect man to sin; it sets forth a principal that argues against such a position. Consider the importance of this fact. Let's imagine for a moment that Camping's statement were true. Wouldn't God go to great

1. Camping, God's Magnificent Salvation 2.

lengths to prove it? Wouldn't He wish to vindicate His justice by communicating to us, in no uncertain terms, that Adam acted not in *accordance* with his nature, but *against* it? Of course He would. *If* such a thing were possible. At the very least He would set forth a principle which would demonstrate how such a thing might happen. But not only does He not do this; He sets forth the very opposite principle. He explicitly states that bad fruit *cannot* come from a good tree. "Either make the tree good; or else make the tree corrupt, and his fruit corrupt: for the tree is known by his fruit." (Matthew 12:32–34) Who planted Adam? God did, of course. How did He sow him? "It is *sown* in corruption." (1 Cor. 15:42) How did that happen? By the creature's sin? "For the creature was subjected to vanity, *not willingly*. . . ." If Camping's justification for eternal torment is true, how can we account for the fact that God seems *completely unaware* of such a possibility?

## 2. We Do Not Have Free Will

Romans 9:19 says "Thou wilt say then unto me, Why doth he yet find fault? For who resisted his will?"

The question is posed after Paul insists that God chose Jacob over Esau before they were even born and hardened Pharaoh in order to show His power throughout the earth. It is in this context that the question is raised. Now, if in fact man had free will of a *relevant* kind, if God had chosen Jacob because He *foresaw* that Jacob, unlike Esau, would *respond* to His calling, or if he hardened Pharaoh because He *foresaw* that Pharoah would harden himself, then this was the perfect opportunity for Paul to reveal precisely this fact. Simply consider how the Arminian would answer that question. Surely by saying something like: "Oh, you misunderstand. He hardens men like Esau and Pharaoh based on His foreknowledge of how they will respond to the gospel. Basically, they are hardening themselves."

Is that how Paul responds? No. He says "Nay but, O man, who art thou that repliest against God? Should the thing formed say to him that formed it, Why hast thou made me thus? Hath not the potter power over the clay, of the same lump to make one vessel unto honour, and another unto dishonour?" And so we see that the principle employed by Arminians to argue their case—namely, free will—is not only not found here, but its opposite is boldly asserted. If God had chosen Jacob over Esau because He had foreseen that Jacob would *accept* Him and Esau wouldn't, then the objection would have never arisen in the first place. It would simply be a matter of fairness. God is rewarding Jacob's faith and punishing Esau's faithlessness. Who could possibly object to that? If an objection did arise to such a decision, it would certainly have taken a different form than the one anticipated by Paul. But look at the words: ". . . *Why* doth he yet find fault?" Remember the old Bud commercial—Why ask why? Well, it's an apt question if Arminianism is true. Why ask why? Why, if God is simply responding to one man's goodness and to the other man's wickedness, is anyone asking *why*?

## 3. God Is Mindful of Our Frame

> "For He knows our frame; He remembers that we are dust." (Psalm 103:14)

> "For the Lord will not cast off forever: But though he cause grief, yet he will have compassion according to the multitude of his mercies. For he does not afflict willingly nor grieve the children of men." (Lam. 3:32–33)

How can anyone of normal understanding, using sound principles of bible interpretation, possibly reconcile these verses with the idea that God created us for the purpose of torturing us forever in hell?

If God does not enjoy imposing even temporal afflictions, then how can He enjoy imposing eternal torment? If He remembers our *finite* frames in accessing penalties, then how can those penalties be *infinite*?

## 4. God Is Our Father

I said . . . all of you are children of the Most High (Ps. 82:6).

You are our Father . . . our potter; and all we are the work of Your hand (Is. 64:8).

Have we not all one Father? Has not one God created us? (Mal. 2:10)

Seeing the multitudes. . . . In this manner pray: our Father . . . (Mt. 5:1; 6:9).

Jesus spoke to the multitudes and to His disciples . . . one is your Father (Mt. 23:1, 9).

Men of Athens. . . . For we also are His children. Being then the children of God . . . (Ac. 17:22, 28–29 NAS).

I bow to the Father . . . from whom the whole family in . . . earth is named (Ep. 3:14–15).

Be in subjection to the Father of spirits and live (He. 12:9)

## 5. God Created Man in His Own Image

God created man in His own image . . . (Ge. 1:27, 9:6).

No-one of normal understanding can understand the making of a creature in one's own image—and then declaring it very good—as consistent with hating that creature and wishing to see it eternally miserable.

## 6. It Is Possible to Lie for God

Job 13:7–8 says: "Will ye speak wickedly for God? And talk deceitfully for him? Will ye accept his person? will ye contend for God?"

If Calvinism is true, then exactly how is it even possible to lie for God? What could you possibly ascribe to Him that is worse than the truth? Could you ascribe to Him a worse motive in creation than the one He actually employed? Could you ascribe to Him less mercy than He actually shows? Greater cruelty? More indifference? What could you possibly say against Him that isn't but a pale reflection of an even more awful truth? One might object that Job represents not man, but Christ. But this objection will not do. After all, who ever claimed that Christ *deserved* His punishment, as Job's "friends" insisted Job deserved his?

## 7. God Sees the Act of Creation as Suggesting a Bond

I have already treated this topic at length; hence I will simply reference the appropriate verses here.

> You are our Father . . . our potter; and all we are the work of Your hand (Is. 64:8).

> Have we not all one Father? Has not one God created us? (Mal. 2:10)

> "Who is the image of the invisible God, the firstborn of every creature: For by him were all things created . . . all things were created by him and for him: And he is before all things, and by him all things consist." (Col. 1:15–17)

"And has made of one blood all nations of men for to dwell on all the face of the earth, and hath determined the times appointed, and the bounds of their habitation; That they should seek the Lord, if haply they might feel after Him, and find Him, though He be not far from every one of us: For in Him we live, and move, and have our being; as certain also of your own poets have said, For we are also *His offspring*." (Acts 17:26–28)

## 8. God Sees a Link between Subjecting Us to Vanity and Releasing Us from It

The Calvinist and the Universalist each employ their own proof text as to why man was created. The Calvinist employs Romans 9:22; the Universalist Romans 8:20.

Romans 9:22–23: "What if God, willing to show his wrath, and to make his power known, endured with much longsuffering the vessels of wrath fitted to destruction: And that he might make known the riches of his glory on the vessels of mercy, which he had afore prepared unto glory."

Romans 8:20–21: "For the creature was made subject to vanity, not willingly, but by reason of him who hath subjected the same, in hope, Because the creature itself also shall be delivered from the bondage of corruption into the glorious liberty of the children of God."

I will now demonstrate that the Calvinist, if he is consistent, must agree with Rom 8:20, while disagreeing with Romans 8:21. The Calvinist believes that in the best of all possible worlds, sin must exist. It must exist because, as Romans 9:22 insists, God must display his glory by punishing it. But if the best of all possible worlds includes sin, then God had to create man not only liable to sin, but *certain* to sin. Hence he had to "make man subject to vanity." But notice the problem. Romans 8:20 insists that God subjected creation to vanity, not, as the Calvinist insists, to punish him for it, but rather to *free* him from it. Vanity was not created as an end in itself, but as a means to an end. And to this the scriptures agree:

"Howbeit that was not first which is spiritual, but that which is natural; and afterward that which is spiritual." (1 Cor 15:46)

"For the Lord will not cast off forever: But though he cause grief, yet he will have compassion according to the multitude of his mercies. For he does not afflict willingly nor grieve the children of men. (Lamentations 3:32–33)

"It is an experience of evil Elohim [God] has given to the sons of humanity to humble them by it." (Concordant Old Testament)

But Calvinists attribute to God an entirely different motive in giving us an "experience of evil"—and an unspeakably fiendish one at that. The Calvinist, therefore, would require that Romans 8:20–21 be rendered this way: "For the creature was made subject to vanity, not willingly, but by reason of him who hath subjected the same, in order to torment them forever in hell." The Calvinist simply cannot establish a logical link between the *way* God made us and the *why*. On the one hand, they insist He made us to punish us, which, to any rational mind, would mean He made us "subject to vanity"; on the other hand, they insist He made us perfect. All Romans 8:20 does is insist on a logical link between the *way* God made us and the *why*.

The Calvinist might raise the objection that he does not believe this verse applies to human beings. No matter. According to his own theology it *does* apply to human beings—at least the first half. His God *had* to make man subject to vanity in order to fulfill His own purposes. We therefore have a verse that perfectly describes the way the Calvinist God *had* to create man, which they say doesn't apply to man because they don't like the next verse!

## 9. Sin against Man Is Sin against God

Proverbs 14:31 says "He who oppresses the poor reproaches his Maker." How can this be true if the Calvinist conception of God is correct? How could God equate sin against man—who He hates—with sin against Him?

## 10. There's No Such Thing as Disinterested Benevolence

Presumably, Adam's great sin was that he put his own desires before his duties to His creator. In other words, he acted selfishly. And to be sure the bible does—and ought to—regard selfishness as a sin, even as we do in secular society. But selfishness is also very natural. All things are driven first and foremost by self-interest. This is true in the very nature of things. It is desirable, of course, that we pursue happiness by way of virtue rather than sin, but even so, our *primary* objective remains the same—happiness; we simply learn to pursue it by different methods. This is particularly important with regard to Calvinism, whereby the essence of sin is to put one's own happiness before God's glory. Ironically, the Calvinist sees nothing wrong with God putting His own glory before the happiness of His own creatures. And why do they suppose He does this? Presumably, because it *makes Him happy.* Or else He wouldn't do it, would He? The right to the pursuit of happiness, therefore, is confined to the creator and denied all others.

Now, here's my point: If pursuing happiness were wrong, then we ought to find that this propensity is fiercely condemned in the bible. Do we? To the contrary, we see the very author and finisher of our faith—Christ Himself—driven by this very same motive. Why did Christ endure the cross? Because it was the right thing to do? No. He endured it "for the joy that was set before him" and that God might "glorify me with thine own self with the glory which I had before the world was." (Heb. 12:2; Jn 17:5). Now, the Calvinist might answer, as I have noted above, that it is okay for Christ—as part of the Godhead—to pursue His own happiness. But even so, was He not acting as the federal head of the human race, and setting Himself forth as an example? We are told to "*Look unto Jesus,* the author and finisher of our faith . . ." (Heb. 12:2). What a bizarre notion that God, who has everything, ought to act out of self interest, whereas man, who has nothing comparatively speaking, ought to act out of disinterested benevolence! How dramatically this idea contradicts the biblical record, which portrays God as one who gives out of an overflow. It is precisely *because* He needs nothing that He is able to give selflessly in a way that could not possibly be expected of a mere mortal. "If I was hungry would I tell you?" (Psalm 50:12) Are we to honestly believe that God condemns us eternally for having a proclivity that results simply from *not being God?*

At any rate, I could set forth even more of these principles, but since my point point is made, I might as well stop here. But consider this fact: I have enumerated not one, not two, not four, but ten principles, which, if traditional church teaching were true, not only ought not to be found in scripture, but ought to be replaced with their opposites. Then why are they found? Is it not presumptive proof that the thing which constrains the Christian church to deny them—eternal torment—is simply not true? The fact is this: An entire conceptual framework, consisting of ideas which are alien to both reason and scripture, had to be invented to justify eternal torment. Doesn't this tell us something? Could it be that the principles just examined comprise *reality* as we know it, and that a world in which their opposites prevailed would not retain the properties of a coherent reality at all? Are there any known principles which might sustain the Calvinist version of reality? Are they communicable by ordinary language? If so, then why are they not found in scripture? Why are the aforementioned principles, which are constantly denied by professionally trained theologians, *never* denied by the authors of the bible? Disregarding these principles, which comprise *reality* as we know it, has led to man-made, unbiblical, illogical, immoral, inhumane, theological constructs which bear no resemblance to reality whatsoever, and are said to be "above reason." Simply try to imagine the nightmarish bizarro world reality that would result if these ten principles were reversed. On the other hand, don't imagine anything. Simply look at the *Calvinist Happy Coincidence* model of sin and salvation.

1.  From eternity past God intended that the most vivid and profound demonstration of his glory would come in the form of His work of salvation on the cross of Christ.

2.  God then made man to punish him

3.  He made him perfect and thus unlikely to ever need punishing, or, for that matter, a savior

4.  By a happy coincidence, and against all the odds, this perfect man sinned, thus allowing God to fulfill His purposes for both the man and Christ

5.  When he sinned, God, who is suddenly confronted with the prospect of being able to fulfill all of His original plans, becomes *furious*

Every step in the process contradicts the one before! Calvinism is the theological equivalent of Alice in Wonderland's rabbit hole—a terrifying abys where the only sense is nonsense. Truly Robin Williams might have had Calvinism in mind when he said "Reality. What a concept!" Which, it just so happens, brings us to our next chapter.

## 5

# Reality: What a Concept!

I WOULD LIKE TO begin this chapter with a quote from C.S. Lewis:

> "Heaven will solve our problems, but not, I think, by showing us subtle reconciliations between all our apparently contradictory notions. The notions will all be knocked from under our feet. We shall see there was never any problem.
>
> "And more than once, that impression which I can't describe except by saying it's like the sound of a chuckle in the darkness. The sense that some shattering and disarming simplicity is the real answer."

The Christian church has always held to the idea that God is simple. This idea, however, cannot be true if Calvinism is correct. We just explored the Calvinist Happy Coincidence model of sin and salvation. Is it not fraught with contradictions that require reconciling? Let's look at it again.

- From eternity past God intended that the most vivid and profound demonstration of his glory would come in the form of His work of salvation on the cross of Christ.

- God then made man to punish him

- He made him perfect and thus unlikely to ever need punishing, or, for that matter, a savior

- By a happy coincidence, and against all the odds, this perfect man sinned, thus allowing God to fulfill His purposes for both the man and Christ

- When he sinned, God, who is suddenly confronted with the prospect of being able to fulfill all of His original plans, becomes *furious*

*This* is the "shattering simplicity" that is the real answer? For the sake of argument, let's assume that it is. The bible says "be ready always to give an answer" (1 Peter 3:15). Can the Calvinists give an answer? One that they honestly believe? Their appeals to mystery clearly indicate that they cannot. But the truth is supposed to erase mystery, not deepen it! How is it that the Calvinists, upon finding truth, must still plead mystery? How is it that the deeper they go into truth, the deeper the mystery becomes? Is the truth really that complicated?

The bible doesn't seem to suggest this at all. To the contrary, it hints at a simple truth. Matthew 11:25 says: ". . . I thank thee, O Father . . . because thou hast hid these things from the wise and prudent, and hast revealed them unto babes." The question is: What is God hiding? Is it something simple? Or something complicated and esoteric? If it's complicated and esoteric, then why would God have any need to hide it? Why would He have to hide something that's beyond human comprehension in the first place? Indeed He *couldn't* hide it. He could choose not to *reveal it*; but He couldn't hide it. The bible, however, suggests a truth that's being hidden. Moreover, it suggests that this truth, far from being beyond our grasp, is actually so evident that God must take great measures to conceal it. Mark 4:12 says that God hides the truth so that "seeing they may see, and not perceive; and hearing they may hear, and not understand; lest at any time they should be converted . . ." This suggests a truth so obvious and so simple that God Himself must blind us to *keep us from repenting*. The same idea is found in Acts 17:26–28:

> "And hath made of one blood all nations of men for to dwell on the face of the earth, and hath determined the times before appointed, and the bounds of their habitation; That they should seek the Lord, if haply they might feel after him, and find him, though he be not far from every one of us. For in him we live, and move, and have our being; as certain of your own poets have said, For we are also his offspring."

Just as in Mark 4:12, we have the image of men groping in the dark, trying to *feel after* that which is right in front of them. Is this darkness meant to continue forever in the case of most of humanity?

> "And he will destroy in this mountain the face of the covering cast over all people, and the vail that is spread over all nations. He will

> swallow up death in victory; and the Lord God will wipe away tears from off all faces . . ." (Is. 25:7–8)

> "Therefore wait ye upon me, saith the Lord, until the day that I rise up to the prey: for my determination is to gather the nations, that I may assemble the kingdoms, to pour upon them mine indignation, even all my fierce anger: for all the earth shall be devoured with the fire of my jealousy. For then I will turn to the people a pure language, that they may all call upon the name of the Lord, to serve him with one consent." (Zephaniah 3:8)

The "all nations" that will worship the Lord in these two verses is the same "all nations of men" that the Lord made from "one blood" in Acts 17. Yes, one day the veil will be lifted for *all* men. All men will see the *simple* truth. The Christian religious system, however, does not see it that way. Shirley C. Guthrie writes:

> Logically, evil is impossible in a world created and ruled by God, for it is just what God did *not* create and does *not* will. This is the parasitical power of evil. It is not the truth about who we are and what the world is like; it is a *lie*, a *contradiction*, and *denial* of the truth. . . . Evil is the Big Lie that is so destructive and terrible just because it convinces us that the truth about God, God's world, and life in it is not the truth."[1]

How appropriate that this quote is from a book entitled Christian Doctrine. It's appropriate because this silliness *is* Christian doctrine. The author admits that evil "*is not who we are.*" And yet, we are to believe that God will keep us trapped forever in a state of existence that *is not who we are*, in order to punish us for *being in that state*. Is it any wonder that the Christian system, while professing that reality is simple, must also depict it as something esoteric and convoluted? It is necessary to sustain their conclusions. Simply consider the Arminian and Calvinist conceptions of reality. One insists that evil is an unwanted intrusion into the universe, for which no explanation can suffice, and for which man is entirely responsible; the other insists that God intended evil, but bears no responsibility for its existence, its consequences, or its duration. These two systems can be summed up this way:

---

1. Guthrie, Christian Doctrine 188.

Arminianism: God, who *could* have done it (created evil), *wouldn't* have done it; therefore man, who *couldn't* have done it, *must* have done it.

Calvinism: God, who needed evil, nonetheless bears no responsibility for its existence; nor did He create man in a manner consistent with His aim; it just sort of happened by a happy coincidence.

These are the only two realities available to most Christians. Like the reality of Alice in Wonderland's rabbit hole, it is one in which the only sense is nonsense. It is a reality where effects do not flow proportionately from causes, things do not operate in accordance with their natures, and the operative factor seems to be a mysterious randomness that "causes" men to act against their own natures, their best interests, and their Creator's designs in ways that do them irreparable harm. Moreover, they are *born* into that condition, yet entirely responsible for it. Hell is the default condition of man. It is what naturally accrues to man merely by virtue of existing. Why? Because our sin—the sin of the frail, finite creature—*infinitely* offends the creator. But this is no indictment of the creator. To the contrary, it is the very fact that God is good that causes this terrible consequence. Indeed it is God's *very character as infinite God* that constitutes infinite peril to His own creation, for it is His very nature—His infinite majesty—that dictates that the slightest sin be punished with eternal torment. God's very nature as infinite good dictates that anything He creates, which, by *its* very nature will be *less* than infinite good, will, on that account, arouse His infinite wrath; hence God, for all practical purposes, *inherently* hates His creatures. Oh, yes there are the elect, whom he doesn't hate. But this is only *supererogatory*; He really *ought* to hate them. Infinite evil, therefore, is the default position for any created intelligence that stems from infinite good. We are born with an inherently negative value. We deserve only misery and torment. Who we are in God, in whose image we were created, and in whom we *live, and move, and have our being* (Acts 17:28) is not the real us; who we are *outside* of God is the *real* us. This is the reality we find ourselves faced with simply by virtue of being born.

Such a reality is a wonderful thing—if you're God! For everyone-else, it's horrific beyond words. How can anyone who believes in *this* reality dare to suggest that evil is a distortion of reality rather than its very essence? If this be the case, then why do we go about our lives as if things make sense? As if up is up rather than down? As if black isn't white and white isn't black? How can we trust our intellects? Our sense of reason? Our consciences?

## Part 1: Is God the Universal Father?

How can anything have any meaning at all? How can we get angry over injustice? Acts of violence? Horrible crimes? Why should we continue to plod along through the motions of life when life itself is arrayed against us in every possible way? When all of our senses are nothing more than mediums of deception and every bit of knowledge has served no other purpose other than to make us more stupid? Who could labor—even for an instant—under such a reality? Is this not presumptive proof that none of us really believe it? If we did, would not the entire world dissolve into a giant insane asylum? Does not the simple fact that our daily lives proceed in accordance with a belief in the reliability of our senses indicate that we do not accept this version of reality? After all, we do not distrust our senses at every turn, do we? Do we think that every single human act is utterly devoid of objective meaning except for the act of *groveling to God?*

Thank God this is not the biblical witness of reality. The bible presents reality as simple, as good, and as consisting of love. And this finds the deepest resonance, and an infallible witness, in the human heart and mind and conscience and God-given senses. We know that it is always better to love than to hate, to forgive than hold a grudge, and to help rather than to hurt. There is never, even for an instant, the sense that this knowledge is somehow the result of misguided senses or a bad conscience. There is never the sense that if we thought as God did we would be *less* loving, less forgiving, less caring. Never. Either God has gone to the greatest possible lengths to deceive us in this regard, or the Christian religious system in general—and Calvinism in particular—has misunderstood reality.

I would also suggest that if they have *not* misunderstood it, then there's no reason for anyone to believe that they *have* understood it. The comedian Steven Wright once joked: "Last night someone broke into my house and replaced all of my furniture with exact replicas." Imagine that the truth really were something esoteric and obscure—something that required enormous discernment to understand. Now further imagine that it was something that God deliberately hid from most men that they might perish for all eternity. If this really is the case, then how can anyone have the temerity to imagine that they have come to truth? For surely even the most profound internal witness of the spirit might be nothing more than a delusion sent by God. If Wright had been ribbing on Calvinists, he might have said: *Last night God broke into my heart and gave me perfect truth that looked exactly like a lie.* The Calvinist truth looks exactly like a lie. Their God looks exactly like the devil. Their logic looks illogical; their love like hate; their good like evil. Moreover, they admit that God hides the truth. But if God hides the truth, and *their* truth looks exactly like a lie, then upon what basis can they say they have found the truth?

But thank God the Calvinist and Arminian versions of reality are not the only ones that exist. I would now like to present an entirely different version of reality. It is the version of reality which we all think, deep down, *should* be true. It is a version which, if eternal torment is true, ought to have no place—even in the form of appearances—in scripture, for surely God ought not to reinforce our delusions.

Let's start at the beginning. With the simple fact that evil exists. Why? Each of the three systems—Arminianism, Calvinism, and Universalism— give a different reason. Arminians suggest that evil is an unwanted intruder in the universe. We don't exactly know how it got here; all we know is that it's here to stay. Calvinism suggests that evil exists so that God may punish it as a demonstration of His justice to the praise of His glory. And Universalism suggests that evil exists as a brief, albeit painful, prelude to eternal glory—part of a process that was conceived without any elements of contingency or malice.

It would seem to me that the first two models both suggest essentially the same thing. They both seem to suggest that if God did not create us perfect from the outset than He must have either been incompetent (Arminianism) or cruel (Calvinism). In other words, neither accepts that God may have created man imperfect as part of a *natural growth process.* I will not pretend to know how a perfect Creator goes about His business, but the idea that He would have made us perfect from the start seems extremely far-fetched. Simply try to picture it. God, the all-mighty, all-sovereign King of the Universe, who is attended at every instant by myriads of angels, whose wisdom and power sustain all things, and reverberates through every fiber of every creature in all of creation, is about to create something in *His own image.* He announces it to the heavenly hosts—"Let us make man in our image"—who respond with breathless anticipation. Now, who in their right senses would imagine—even for an instant—that God is about to embark upon a creative act whose entire scope and character will be over the instant it begins, with the result being myriads of intelligent beings shining forth the full radiance of God, complete in their knowledge of their Creator's attributes, and quivering with joy over the blessedness of their estate in Christ? It is unthinkable, and perhaps on that account quite suited to those who don't *think.*

## Part 1: Is God the Universal Father?

The alternative, of course, is to involve man in a process. This means to create him less than perfect. And imperfection, as any Calvinist knows, is *evil*. And once you make imperfection necessary, you make sin necessary. And once you make sin necessary, you make it *finite*. God cannot be infinitely offended by that which He brings to pass. Nor can an imperfect man possess a perfect *appreciation* of God's perfect law; hence the sin *cannot* be infinite.

Here's where things get tricky. They get tricky because the Calvinist, to a very large extent, does not dispute the premise here outlined. They admit that sin must exist in the best of all possible worlds. They just don't believe it exists for the same reasons the Universalists do. The Calvinist believes that the best of all possible worlds is one in which God maximally displays all of His attributes. Justice, of course, is one of His attributes. God, therefore, had to create vessels of wrath to punish, thereby displaying His justice. Hence, we have something of a stalemate, with something of a stalemate. Both the Calvinist and the Universalist accept the idea that sin must exist in the best of all possible worlds. The Universalist gives his reasons; the Calvinists gives his. As is often the case with these two camps, they are simply doing different dances to the same music! How do we know whose doing the right dance?

Let me propose a way to decide. Let us accept the proposition that God wishes to maximally display all of His attributes. Let us further suppose that God never planned to send a single soul to hell. Would God have *still* had to create man imperfect in order to maximally display His attributes? Could a perfect, pristine universe, untouched by corruption of any kind, have afforded God the opportunity to maximally display His glory to His creatures? And is it likely that He would have *wanted* to display that glory simply by creating men perfect and instilling in us, at the moment of our conception, a perfect knowledge of all things?

If the answer to either of these questions is no, then the Calvinists have a dilemma on their hands. God, in order to maximally display His glory, had to make man imperfect *even if He never planned to send a single soul to hell*. Then why, when a perfectly good motive naturally exists for making man imperfect, would they want to ascribe to Him such a perfectly *awful* motive? Indeed it is the very fact that God wishes to maximally display His attributes that all but dictates that He would do it by way of a *natural growth process*. And so the *very motive the Calvinist employ to suggest that God made us for hell*—His need to maximally display His attributes—is the *very same thing* that makes it extremely unlikely that He would have made us perfect from the start. We can plainly see, therefore, that the very foundation of Calvinist thought—the idea that if God allowed sin, then it must have been in order to punish it forever—entails a positively stupefying travesty of logic.

The fact is that God, in order to display His attributes, had to create, not sin and punishment, as the Calvinists insist, but corruption and vanity, as the bible insists. His strength is perfected in . . . what? *Weakness.* (2 Cor. 12:9) And how was man created? ". . . it is sown in weakness . . ." (1 Cor. 15:43) In other words, God had to create for man an environment where the attributes of Christ could flourish. The bible never says that God's goal in creation was sin and punishment. But what does it say?

> "For the creature was made subject to vanity, not willingly, but by reason of him who hath subjected the same, in hope, Because the creature itself also shall be delivered from the bondage of corruption into the glorious liberty of the children of God."

Man's imperfect nature allows for a demonstration that would have otherwise been impossible. To reduce this demonstration to nothing more than God's mercy, as shown in vessels of mercy, and justice, as shown in vessels of wrath, is incredibly simplistic and fails to consider the broader picture. There are *many* things on display in this world besides mercy and punishment. What about contrast? The chance to observe and experience the *difference* between things? Did not Adam eat from a tree whose fruit contained the knowledge of *both* good and evil? And what about Christ Himself? Hebrews 8:5 says even Christ "learned obedience by things which he suffered." How could He have suffered anything in a world without evil? Christ Himself is proof positive that God had to make man "subject to vanity" even if He never planned to send a single soul to hell.

But of course all of this is mere conjecture if the scripture does not back it up. Does it? Quite explicitly. 1 Cor. 15:46 states the matter clearly and concisely: "Howbeit that was not first which was spiritual, but that which is natural; and afterward that which is spiritual." There is the natural growth process. It is from the natural to the spiritual. If anyone would suggest that the word *natural* does not denote evil of any kind, I would merely refer them to the subsequent verses.

> "So also is the resurrection of the dead. It is sown in corruption; it is raised in incorruption: It is sown in dishonour; it is raised

in glory; it is sown in weakness; it is raised in power: It is sown a natural body; it is raised a spiritual body. There is a natural body, and there is a spiritual body. And so it is written, The first man Adam was made a living soul; the last Adam was made a quickening spirit."

These verses give the lie to the Arminian idea that corruption is an unwanted intruder into God's holy universe, and to the Calvinist idea that it was created as an end in itself. This was God's plan of creation; it was not an *accomodtion* to unwanted events, as the Arminians would suggest; nor was it enacted with malice, as the Calvinists suggest. It is simply the way God ordained that things would proceed—by stages. It is exactly the way we would *expect* a perfect Creator to create. It is a reality that makes sense. And this is what it all comes down to, isn't it? If the bible, as the Christian system suggests, insists on a *different* kind of reality than the one that we would expect from a perfect Creator, then why do so many verses seem to give us exactly the one we *do* expect? We would *expect* the One who imprisons us all in disobedience to release us from it. What does the bible say?

"For God hath concluded all in unbelief, that he might have mercy upon all." (Rom 11:32)

We would *expect* the One who condemned us in Adam to justify us in Christ. What does the bible say?

"Therefore as by the offense of one judgment came upon all men to condemnation; even so by the righteousness of one the free gift came upon all men unto justification of life." (Rom 5:18)

We would *expect* that the One who killed us in Adam will make us alive in Christ. What does the bible say?

"As in Adam all die, so shall all be made alive in Christ." (1 Cor. 15:22)

And most of all, we would *expect,* as a matter of fairness, that there exists a relationship between our current condition of vanity and our future state. What does the bible say?

"For the creature was made subject to vanity, not willingly, but by reason of Him who hath subjected the same, in hope, because the creature itself also shall be delivered from the bondage of corruption into the glorious liberty of the children of God." (Rom. 8:20–21)

We see by these verses that the bible emphatically endorses a reality that actually makes sense. How can we explain this if the Calvinist or Arminian realities were true? How can the bible offer so many verses that resonate with everything we think *should* be true if in fact the opposite is true? Was God trying to be politically correct? If He thinks *so* differently than we do about these matters of fundamental fairness, then why does His language suggest just the opposite? Why didn't He simply dispel our illusions with verses like:

> For God hath concluded all in unbelief, that He might have mercy on *some*. Or,

> As in Adam all die, so in Christ shall *some* be made alive. Or,

> Therefore as by the offense of the one judgment came upon all men to condemnation; even so by the righteousness of one the free gift came upon *a few men* unto justification of life." Or,

> For the creature was made subject to vanity, not willingly, but by reason of him who hath subjected the same, in hope, because the creature itself also shall be *tormented forever in hell*.

At this point the Calvinist might respond: God can phrase things any way He wants to; He doesn't owe man anything. But this merely begs the question. The above mentioned verses seem to suggest that God, having subjected man to vanity, *does* owe him something—a release from it. But does it really matter what God does or doesn't owe us? First off, the verses themselves clearly indicate that God's will was the decisive force in death, disobedience, vanity, etc. . . . And secondly, even if we deny this and put the blame on man, we must still confront the language of these verses. Can we really argue that it's okay for God to make a false promise just so long as He doesn't really *owe* us the thing promised?

The fact is that the verses say what they say and we should *all* hope that they *mean* what they say. If they don't, then we are all stuck in a terrifying and illogical reality. This illogical reality is reflected in all of the major doctrines of the Christian religious system. We will take a closer look at these doctrines in the next section.

# PART 2

## Two Gods: Two Sets of Doctrines

JOHN PIPER WRITES: "THE practical issues at stake in any one intellectual controversy are almost always more than we realize. This is especially true where fundamentally contrary views of God are in conflict. When the paths diverge at the top, almost everything will be different."[1]

Certain conclusions flow naturally from certain premises. These conclusions then harden into the doctrines that form the basis for a particular theological system. Having diverged at the top, Calvinism and Universalism have, not surprisingly, developed two very different sets of doctrines. The root of that divergence can be easily discerned by even a cursory glance at each system's primary proof text. Calvinism derives its understanding of the character of God and his purpose in creation from Romans 9:22: "What if God, willing to show his wrath, and to make his power known, endured with much longsuffering the vessels of wrath fitted to destruction: And that he might make known the riches of his glory on the vessels of mercy, which he had afore prepared unto glory."

God has done his creatures no wrong by fitting them for destruction; indeed God, by definition, *can* do no wrong due to the fact that the dictates of His will, however mysterious, are always necessarily just; hence justice, as we might understand it, has no claims on God. That is the root

1. Quote taken from Thomas Talbott's *The Inescapable Love of God* 43.

of Calvinism—the inscrutableness of the Creator. Other doctrines that flow naturally, or, in some cases, I shall argue, unnaturally, from this are as follows:

- A Perfect man named Adam sinned
- We all sinned in Adam
- We die because we sin
- The wages of sin is eternal torment, which Christ paid in order to appease the Father's wrath
- God's supererogatory grace will extend only to the elect

All of these doctrines stress the severity of sin, place the onus of it on man, and relieve God of all responsibility in the matter.

Universalism, on the other hand, finds the fullest expression of its philosophy in Romans 8:20–21: "For the creature was made subject to vanity, not willingly, but by reason of him who hath subjected the same, in hope, Because the creature itself also shall be delivered from the bondage of corruption into the glorious liberty of the children of God."

The Universalist contends that God subjected man to vanity, not that it might give God a chance to showcase his justice by punishing sin, but in order to give man "an experience of evil, that he might be humbled by it" (Ecclesiastes 3:10). Evil is not an end in itself, but a means to an end. Doctrines that follow from this philosophy are:

- An *imperfect* man named Adam sinned
- God imputed the *punishment* of his sin—death—to all men
- We sin because we die (our mortality makes us weak)
- The wages of sin is death, which Christ paid, not to appease an angry God, but to appease our own hostility toward God
- God's grace will eventually extend to all men

The doctrines of Universalism stress God's sovereignty over the human will and the corrective nature of all discipline.

This section of the book will take each of these doctrines in order.

# 6

# Adam and Eve

THE STORY OF ADAM and Eve presents us with five interesting facts:

1. God has made man in His image

2. God knows good and evil

3. He places Adam and Eve in a garden with a tree. It is a tree of the knowledge of good and evil.

4. He tells them not to eat from it.

5. He has Satan tempt them to eat from it.

Did God set them up? Did he want them to eat from the tree? Well, it certainly *seems* like He did. God, who knows good and evil, creates man, who does *not* know good from evil. He creates him in His *own image*. And then places before them, in the closest possible proximity, a tree of what? The knowledge of *good and evil*. Then He sends Satan into the garden to tempt them into eating of the tree. Finally, He tells them not to eat of the fruit. In other words, He gives them a law. And what is the purpose of the law? It is to create *disobedience* (Rom. 3:20). Again, it sure does *seem* like God wanted them to eat of the fruit of the tree. It's what any reasonable person would have to infer from the facts.

We have been taught, however, that God did not want the very result that He seemed to go out of his way to get. Why do people tell us this? It's very simple. Because God told them *not* to eat of the fruit of the tree. We know God did not want them to eat the fruit because He told them not to. That's what we've been taught; that's where traditional Christian teaching has left it. A command was given; it was disobeyed, and the rest is history. End of story.

Not so fast. Let's say—just for the sake of argument—that God *did* want them to eat the fruit. How could He get them to do so? Let's look at the nature of the tree. It is a tree whose fruit is the knowledge of good and evil. How do you eat such a fruit? There is only one way. By sinning. You can only eat from the fruit of the tree of the knowledge of good and evil by sinning. What does this mean? Simple. If God had told them to eat the fruit, and they obeyed, they would not really be eating it. They would simply be eating a piece of fruit. The fruit could only have had an effect if eaten in violation of a command. Therefore, if God *did* want them to eat the fruit, he would have had to tell them *not to*. That leaves us with two possibilities:

1. God did not want them to eat the fruit, in which case He would have told them not to.

2. God did want them to eat the fruit, in which case He would have told them not to.

In either case the command would have been the same; hence we cannot determine God's intent based on the command. We must look at other factors to determine God's intent. We have already noted that the law was given to increase sin, not to prevent it. Does that necessarily mean that God *wanted* them to eat the fruit? It all depends. Of course the law arouses sin in those who are sinners; the question is: Was Adam a sinner before he sinned? Three verses have been employed to argue that he was not. The most oft-cited is Eccl. 7:29. The passage reads:

> "And I find more bitter than death the woman, whose heart is snares and nets, and her hands as bands . . . behold, this have I found . . . counting one by one, to find the account: which yet my soul seeketh, but I find not: one man among a thousand have I found; but a woman among all those have I not found. Lo, this only have I found, that God hath made man upright; but they have sought out many inventions."

There are three things to consider here. First, the preacher precedes his statement about man being made upright by saying that all women are bad. That should give us at least some pause before we decide to take every word of this passage in their most literal sense. Secondly, the statement about men being upright is part of a larger diatribe about humanity in general. Thirdly, the emphasis of the diatribe is not man's uprightness, but man's rottenness. He's including the part about uprightness as a positive in order to stress the negative. In other words, he's saying: *People suck.* They really suck. I've seen them all and I'm here to tell you, they suck. Just plain suck. All of them. Men suck. Women suck—women *really* suck. But they all suck. God made us good, but we really suck.

It is astonishing to think that such a verse has been used as a cornerstone to build the doctrine of man's original perfection.

Another verse employed to support this doctrine is Ezekiel 28:12–15:

> "Son of man, take up a lamentation upon the king of Tyrus, and say unto him, Thus says the Lord God; Thou seal up the sum, full of wisdom, and perfect in beauty. You have been in Eden the garden of God; every precious stone was your covering, the sardius, topaz, and the diamond, the beryl, the onyx, and the jasper, the sapphire, the emerald, and the carbuncle, and gold: the workmanship of your tabrets and of your pipes was prepared in you in the day that you were created. You are the anointed cherub that covers; and I have set you so; you were upon the holy mountain of God; you have walked up and down in the midst of the stones of fire. You were perfect in your ways from the day that you were created, till iniquity was found in you . . ."

It should be noted that opinions differ as to who is actually in view in this verse; some say it's Satan, some say Adam. Gary Cottington gives the following interpretation:

> "*Eden the garden of God*: Not only was Eden the birthplace of mankind, Eden was also a town on the middle Euphrates River that was taken by the Assyrians (2 Kings 19:12; Isaiah 37:12), and was engaged in prosperous trade relations with Tyre (see Ezekiel 27:23). "Eden" is also sometimes used as a symbolic representation of the land of Israel (Isaiah 51:3; Lamentations 2:6; Joel 2:3).
>
> *The mountain of God*: The Hebrew word for mountain, or mount . . . is indicative of Mt. Zion, or Jerusalem (Isaiah 2:2; Micah 4:2; Zephaniah 3:11).
>
> *The covering of precious stones*: most likely refers to the breastplate of precious stones on which the names of the twelve tribes were inscribed as seals (Exodus 28:9–21; 39:10–13). But it is also possible that the precious stones refer to the Torah, which is often evaluated and preferred to them.
>
> Stones of Fire may refer to the stones on the altar of the entire Temple area itself (2 Chronicles 3:6).

The anointed cherub that covers: The Hebrew may indicate that the King of Tyre (the annointed cherub) once served in some sort of protective capacity (a "covering") for the nation of Israel.

Anointed: in the sense of expansion (i.e. with outstretched wings)

Cherub: of uncertain derivative; a cherub or imaginary figure

Covers: properly to entwine as a screen; by implication to fence in, cover over (figuratively) protect

Friendly relations between Tyre and Israel went as far back as the days of Kings David and Solomon, who purchased cedar from Phoenician King Hiram for the building of the temple (1 Kings 5:2–11). Tyre, which also had a formidable army (see Ezekiel 27:10), stood with Israel as an ally against both the Assyrians and the Babylonians . . .

After a thorough examination of this passage in context, we offer the explanation that Tyre, after its long and friendly association with Israel, became rich by its trade and haughty as a result. Tyre spurned this relationship with lowly Israel because its concern was to "heap up riches." It became corrupt in its trade until finally, in the person of one of its royal members, it was cast out of the Temple, and out of the land, which ended the long and friendly relationship between Judah and Tyre.

Tyre is also used as a symbolic representation of the Harlot Church, Babylon the Great, and her impending judgment [Compare Ezekiel 27 & 28 with Revelation 18]."[1]

For the sake of argument, however, we will assume the passage is referring to Adam. Is this verse indicating that Adam was created a perfect spiritual being with little or no capacity for sin—a kind of co-equal with God who, of his own volition, decided to rebel?

I doubt it. A perfectly natural interpretation is this: Adam was made in the image of God, glorious in every way, except one—he was flesh and blood.

". . . The first Adam was made a living soul; the last Adam was made a quickening spirit." (1 Cor 15:45)

"Howbeit that was not first which is spiritual, but that which is natural; and afterward that which is spiritual." (1 Cor. 15: 46)

1. Cottington, "The Lucifer Myth."

Just as Christ was the second Adam, so Adam was the first Christ; in that sense he was glorious. He was the first draft of perfection; Christ, however, was the prototype.

It's also noteworthy that this verse can also be used *against* the Perfect Adam theory. Note the language: "You were perfect . . . till iniquity was *found in you*." How do you find something that wasn't already there? And what is the purpose of the law? To *reveal* sin (Rom. 3:20). Moreover, 1 Cor.15:42–47 clearly indicates that man was *created* an earthy being; there's no suggestion that it occurred as a result of sin. A person can start out "perfect" and still be subject to death and decay. Newborn babies are proof.

Another verse employed in defense of the Perfect Adam theory is James 1:13: "Let no man say when he is tempted, I am tempted of God: for God cannot be tempted with evil, neither tempteth he any man . . ." This verse, however, is in no way addressing the likelihood of Adam sinning; it's merely saying that God didn't tempt him to sin. But what exactly constitutes temptation? When *we* tempt, or when *Satan* tempts, it is not done in the best interests of the object of the temptation. It is a malicious act, designed to harm. In this respect, even if God *did* tempt Adam, the intent of the temptation would be entirely different, given that God intended the temptation for Adam's ultimate good. It is a fact, however, that God did not tempt Adam. Satan did. But God clearly moved Satan to do it, even as he moved Satan to destroy Job (Job 2:3).[2] God cannot tempt, so He had to create someone to do it. He had to create a *tempter*. God cannot *do* evil, so He must create it.

> "I form the light, and create darkness: I make peace and create evil . . ." (Isa. 45:7)
>
> ". . . his hand hath formed the crooked serpent." (Job 26:13)

This is no small distinction. To do evil implies that the evil flows from the person's nature. Evil does not flow from God's nature; He creates it for the purpose of testing man. It does, however, flow from Satan's nature: "When he speaketh a lie, he speaketh of his own . . ." (Jn. 8:44). Preston Eby writes:

> "The Word of God . . . has something to say about what Satan is and *why he is what he is.* . . . Out of God's own mouth proceeds the assertion, "I have created the *waster* to destroy" (Isa. 54:16).

---

2. The verse says Satan moved God, but the context makes clear that God initiated the proceedings.

> We gather from this passage that Satan is a created being with
> a definite purpose. . . . You never thought of Satan as having a
> *ministry*? "Then was Jesus led up of the Spirit into the wilderness
> to be *tempted* (tested) *of the devil*. . . . (Mat. 4:1–2) "Fear none of
> those things which you suffer: behold, the Devil, shall cast some
> of you into prison, *that you may be tried*. . . . (Rev. 2:10) "And
> the Lord said, Simon, Simon, behold, Satan has desired to have
> you, *that he may sift you as wheat*. . . . (Luke 22:31) "Be sober, be
> vigilant; because your adversary the Devil, as a roaring lion, walks
> about, *seeking whom he may devour*: whom resist steadfast in the
> faith, knowing that the same *afflictions* are accomplished in your
> brethren that are in the world" (1 Pet. 5:8–9)."[3]

I would add one more to this list: "To deliver such a one unto Satan
for the destruction of the flesh, that the spirit may be saved in the day of the
Lord Jesus Christ" (1 Cor. 5:5).

Satan is not God's adversary; he is man's adversary. He is God's servant.
God uses him to test man—through temptation. Satan *tempts*; God *tests*.

Those are the three verses used to defend the perfect Adam theory,
and, as we have seen, they are flimsy at best. It is unfortunate that this version of the Adam story has prevailed. It has corrupted our understanding
not only of how things began, but of how things will end. Orthodox Christian teaching ends in an eternal dualism. Both good and evil exist forever.
This vision of an dualistic end can be traced back to a vision of a dualistic
beginning. All things were not created by and for God, nor are all things
headed *to* God; He is not the source *and* the destination, the beginning *and*
the end, the alpha *and* the omega (1 Col. 16, Rom. 11:36, Rev. 1:8). The
mystery of God's will is not, as God's word insists, "to gather all in one,"
and "reconcile all to Himself" and to be "all in all" and have "every tongue
confess" (Eph. 1:9–10, Col. 1:15–20, 1 Cor. 15:28, Phil. 2:10). Instead, the
"mystery" of God's "hidden" will—as the Calvinists call it—is to keep evil
alive forever in a corner of the universe called hell. Instead of a current of
history that is moving inexorably toward unity in Christ, we are told that
good and evil will move in parallel lines for all eternity.

We have been given a picture that pits man against God—as a kind
of co-equal—right from the very beginning. We were created, that much is
true. But we were created so perfectly, with such autonomy, that whatever
happened after that was enough to cancel out the fact that we were created
in Christ. This autonomy was so profound as to place on our shoulders

3. Preston Eby, "The Serpent."

the weight of eternity; one wrong move—literally—and we would be set forever off-course, destined to drift away into eternal darkness, lost and alone, without hope, for as long as God shall live. We were created in and by Christ, but so much *like* Christ, as to have the power to eternally sever ourselves from Him by one wrong move. This was the curse of being created immortal, glorious, perfect, spiritual beings. This is the picture painted for us by the orthodox Christian religious system. Every good "bible believing" Christian has had to accept that his frailness, his depravity, his crookedness, his helplessness, was all the result of a perfect spiritual condition gone horribly wrong—through every fault of his own. An eternal sin with eternal consequences. Perfect Adam made a wrong turn, and drove most of humanity beyond the reach of God forever and ever. An eternal sin in the past; an eternal punishment in the future. This is our lot, our penalty for ruining our perfect, immortal souls. So we've been told.

But is this what the bible really teaches? Let's go back to the beginning. Genesis 2:7 states: "And so it is written, The first Adam was made a living soul." A soul. A living soul. A perfect living soul. A perfect, glorious, immortal living soul. Such are the ideas the word evokes. But do those ideas come from the bible? Or do they come from what we've been taught about the soul? You will notice this passage says nothing about the glorious nature of a soul. A soul, according to the bible, is this: a body plus God's breath. These two things make a soul. David J. Heintzman writes:

> "The Hebrew word for 'soul' in Genesis 2:7 is *nephesh* and occurs four times prior to Genesis 2:7 in the Hebrew text.
>
> And God said, Let the waters bring forth abundantly the moving *creature* (Heb. Nephesh) that hath life, and fowl that may fly above the earth in the open firmament of heaven. Gen 1:20
>
> And God created great whales, and every living *creature* (Heb. Nephesh) that moveth, which the waters brought forth abundantly, after their kind, and every winged fowl after his kind: and God saw that it was good. Gen 1:21
>
> And God said, Let the earth bring forth the living *creature* (Heb. Nephesh) after his kind, cattle, and creeping thing, and beast of the earth after his kind: and it was so. Gen. 1:24
>
> And to every beast of the earth, and to every fowl of the air, and to every thing that creepeth upon the earth, wherein there is life (Heb. Nephesh), I have given every green herb for meat: and it was so. Gen. 1:30

So we see that in these three verses, birds, fish, and animals are also 'souls' as far as the Hebrew use of the word goes."[4]

The fact is that the soul, far from distinguishing us from the animals, actually identifies us with them. This fact is actually a source of frustration to man—a frustration to which man has been subjected by *God Himself* (Rom. 8:20). The theme of this frustration runs through the book of Ecclesiastes. Solomon laments: "I said in my heart concerning the estate of the sons of men, that God might manifest them, and that they might see that they themselves are but beasts . . . so that a man hath no preeminence above a beast: for all is vanity" (Eccl. 3:18). The bible draws strong parallels between man and animals.

Eccl. 3:19 "They all have one breath" (man and animals).

Gen. 3:7 "And the Lord formed man from the dust of the ground, and breathed into his nostrils the breath of life; and man became a living soul."

Orthodox Christian teaching has it backwards. According to them, we were were created immortal, spiritual creatures who, due to sin, were then plunged into a lowly, fleshly condition. But that's not what the bible teaches. There is an order to God's creation, and man did not usurp that order by his sin.

Howbeit that was not first which is spiritual, but that which is natural; and afterward that which is spiritual (1 Cor. 15: 45–46)

It is sown a natural body; it is raised a spiritual body (1 Cor. 15:44)

It is sown in dishonor; it is raised in glory: it is sown in weakness; it is raised in power (1 Cor. 15:43)

It is sown in corruption; it is raised in incorruption (1 Cor 15:42)

L. Ray Smith writes: "Man is not a "spiritual being" having a physical experience, but rather man is a "physical and mortal being" having a "spiritual experience." We are first born mortal (physical), but in the resurrection God gives us immortality (the spiritual) . . ."[5]

In the same vain, Ken Eckerty writes:

"Orthodoxy teaches that Adam was created in a perfect (complete) state. . . . I strongly suggest that this is not true. Ps. 8:5 gives us a

4  David J. Heintzman, *Man Became A Living Soul*, ch 1.

5.  Smith, "Twelve God-Given Truths to Understand His Word."

hint of man's incompleteness: *For thou hast made him a little lower than the angels. . . .* The Hebrew word for "lower" is *chacer* which literally means "to lack" or "fail." Adam . . . lacked something. When Jesus was asked about the resurrection, He said this: *The sons of this age are given in marriage—but they who are worthy to obtain that age, and the resurrection of the dead . . . are equal to the angels . . . (Luke 20:34–36). . . .* Ps. 8:5 tells us that man was made *lower* than the angels, yet Jesus tells us that the sons of God will be *equal* to the angels. In addition, Adam's name literally means "the red earth." While Adam was formed from the dust of the earth, God's destiny for those now "in Adam" is heavenly, not earthly. The problem with the orthodox view is that most Christians believe that God is bringing man back to what Adam originally had in the garden, but the truth is God is bringing man forward to something higher and better."[6]

The thrust of the orthodox argument is that Adam somehow acted in violation of his own perfect nature, thus incurring the terrible penalty. But the bible does not allow for this, for it always affirms that all things—including God and Satan—act in accordance with their natures (Jn. 8:44, Heb. 6:18). This is clearly stated in Matthew 12:33: "Either make the tree good, and his fruit good; or else make the tree corrupt, and his fruit corrupt: for the tree is known by its fruit." Good does not come from bad. The same principle is stated in Matthew 15:18: ". . . those things which proceed out of the mouth come forth from the heart."

This brings us to a very convincing proof that Adam had to sin. He did. The fact that Adam sinned is proof positive that he had to sin. We can prove this by employing the very logic that orthodox theologians use to implicate all men in original sin. We are all sinners, they say, due to the fact that had any one of *us* been in Adam's place, we too would have sinned. This means we cannot put the blame on Adam. He simply did what we all would have done had we been in his shoes. What does such reasoning prove if not the fact that mankind is inherently sinful? Our behavior flows from our nature. Just as surely as every duck quacks and every dog barks and every bird flies, so every man sins. Now if we could in fact find some—or even one duck—that doesn't quack, or one dog that doesn't bark, or one bird that doesn't fly, then our case would collapse. But of course such an exception (apart from some kind of disorder) cannot be found. That's because of the simple fact that everything acts in accordance with its nature. Man is no

6. Eckerty, "Does Man Have Free Will?"

exception. Neither were Adam and Eve, as a comparison of the following verses illustrates.

> 1 John 2:15–16: "Love not the world, neither the things that are in the world. If any man love the world, the love of the father is not in him. For all that is in the world, the lust of the flesh, and the lust of the eyes, and the boastful pride of life, is not of the Father, but is of the world."

> Genesis 2:6: "And when the woman saw that the tree was good for food, and that it was pleasant to the eyes, and a tree to be desired to make one wise, she took of the fruit thereof."

Notice the parallel: "And the woman saw the tree was good for food (the lust of the flesh), and that it was pleasant to the eyes (the lust of the eyes), and a tree to be desired to make one wise (the boastful pride of life) . . ." Gary Cottington writes:

> "The tree of the knowledge of good and evil is the *world*, which is "in the midst of the garden of God," the focal point of God's creation. And all that this world has to offer (the lust of the eyes, the lust of the flesh, and the pride of life) is its *fruit*! "Eden" is symbolic of our innocent, child-like condition. But as we mature and gain knowledge, we lose our innocence and are cast out of this garden paradise (our child-like fantasy world). Now we come to understand that we must learn to "till the ground" and earn our living "by the sweat of our brow," because our parents aren't always going to be there to provide for us. And later in life, when we come to understand our own mortality, we are seduced into thinking (represented by the serpent) . . . that we shall *not* surely die. And this seducing spirit takes many forms, and continues to crawl upon its belly feasting upon *us*, the *dust* of the earth (Genesis 3:19, Ecclesiastes 3:20). And we continue to take refuge in these various forms of religious systems, or coverings (fig leaves), hiding from the truth. But the coverings that we attempt to provide for ourselves are but *illusions*, while God's remedy is sure: "Also for Adam and his wife [and for *all* of humanity as well] the Lord made tunics of skin, and clothed them." (Genesis 3:21)[7]

There's no need to plead mystery here, as theologians typically do when asked how Adam and Eve could have sinned. The bible spells it out in terms simple enough for a child to understand. They sinned out of their

7. Cottington, "Genesis Reloaded Part 4."

own nature. Romans 8:7 says "The carnal mind is enmity against God, for it is not subject to the law of God, neither indeed can be." Adam and Eve, who were made "earthy," and "subject to vanity," were given the *law of God*—"thou shalt not eat"—and the result was this: "And when the woman saw that the tree was good for food, and that it was pleasant to the eyes, and a tree to be desired to make one wise, she took of the fruit thereof" (Genesis 2:6). The law *revealed* their sin. The following two verses, taken together, tell us all we need to know about mankind and sin.

> 1 Cor. 15:53-54: "For this corruptible must put on incorruption, and this mortal must put on immortality. So when this corruptible shall have put on incorruption, and this mortal shall have put on immortality, then shall be brought to pass the saying that is written, Death is swallowed up in victory."

> Romans 8:20-21: "For the creature was made subject to vanity, not willingly, but by Him who subjected the same, in hope, because the creature itself also shall be delivered from the bondage of corruption into the glorious liberty of the children of God."

## One Story—Two Versions

There are many versions of the Adam and Eve story and it seems as if no two of them completely agree. Some insist Adam was made perfect and that sin is a mystery. Others believe that he was created mortal, but with a very low likelihood for sin. Others believe that Adam was created in much the same form—and with all of the same liabilities—as you and me. Still others regard the entire story as a parable. I'm inclined toward the latter view. In any case, there are many different versions of this one story of how it all began. There is also a great deal of overlap among advocates of different theological positions. For the sake of clarity, however, we will compare and contrast the two versions that appear on the farthest ends of the spectrum. We will call designate the first—or traditional viewpoint—*Perfect Adam*, and the opposing view *Poor Adam*. We will look at the differences between the two perspectives with regard to six points, namely:

1. How Adam was created

2. Why he was created

3. Why he fell

4. How he fell

5. Who was responsible

6. How it would be rectified

## 1. How Was Adam Created?

*Perfect Adam* Adam was created perfect. Supporting verses:

- God made man upright (Eccl. 7:29)

- Let us make man in our image . . . (Genesis 1:26)

- You were perfect in your ways from the day that you were created . . . (Ezekiel 28)

*Poor Adam* God made Adam of the earth, corruptible and mortal, the same as the animals. Supporting verses:

- And the Lord formed man of the dust of the ground, and breathed into his nostrils the breath of life, and man became a living soul." (Genesis 2:7)

- ". . . the first man is of the earth, earthy . . ." (1 Cor. 15:47)

- " . . . It is sown in corruption; it is raised in incorruption . . ." (1 Cor. 15:42)

- "The creature was made subject to vanity, not willingly, but by Him who subjected it . . ." (Romans 8:20)

## 2. Why Was Adam Created?

*Perfect Adam* Adam was created to live forever in peace and harmony with Eve and the animals. Unfortunately, he sinned and therefore had to die. Supporting verses:

- "But of the tree of the knowledge of good and evil, thou shalt not eat of it: for in the day that thou eatest thereof thou shalt surely die." (Genesis 2:17)

- "The wages of sin is death." (Romans 6:23)

*Poor Adam* Adam was created mortal in order that—through trials and tribulations—he would learn certain lessons and develop certain attributes on his way to becoming an immortal, spiritual being conformed to the image of Christ (the second Adam). Supporting verses:

- "Howbeit that was not first which was spiritual, but that which is natural; and afterward that which was spiritual. The first man is of the earth, earthy: the second man is the Lord from Heaven." (1 Cor. 15:46–47)
- "I have seen the travail, which God hath given to the sons of men to be exercised in it." (Eccl. 3:10)

### 3. Why Did Adam Fall?

*Perfect Adam* Adam fell due to his desire to be like God. Supporting verses:

> ". . . that when Eve saw that the tree was good for food, and that it was pleasant to the eyes, and a tree to be desired to make one wise, she took of the fruit thereof, and did eat . . ." (Genesis 2:6)

*Poor Adam* Adam fell due to his desire to be like God. In this respect he wanted what God wanted for him. The problem is that he wanted it right away and on his own terms—the way children always want "grown-up" things for which they are not yet ready. And just like a child, he impulsively grabbed for what he wanted. He got what he wanted and found out—surprise—that it was more than he could handle. He was stuck with it and all of the consequences it would bring. God would eventually bring about what Adam tried to bring about himself, but He would do it in His own way and in His own time. A similar theme recurs in Exodus when Moses, zealous for his people's freedom, commits a murder. Moses would indeed free his people, but not before learning a tremendous lesson in humility and patience. Supporting verses:

> "Now the man Moses was very meek, above all the men which were on the face of the earth." (Numbers 12:3)

### 4. How Could Adam Fall? (How Does Perfection Produce Imperfection?)

*Perfect Adam* It's a mystery. Supporting verses:

> "The secret things belong to the Lord . . ." (Deuteronomy 29:29)

*Poor Adam* Adam sinned because he was a sinner. He was fleshly and subject to corruption. Sin was *found* in him (Ezek. 28) because it was already there, waiting to be revealed by the law (Romans 3:20). It was already stirring in him—and her—*before* they ate of the tree: ". . . that when Eve saw that the tree was good for food (the lust of the flesh), and that it was pleasant to the eyes (the lust of the eyes), and a tree to be desired to make one wise (the boastful pride of life) . . ." (Gen. 3:6, 1 John 2:15–16) Moreover, Matthew 12:32–34 tells us in no uncertain terms that evil cannot come from good. Supporting verses:

- "You were perfect . . . until iniquity was found in you." (Ezekiel 28)

- "Love not the world, neither the things that are in the world. If any man love the world, the love of the father is not in him. For all that is in the world, the lust of the flesh, and the lust of the eyes, and the boastful pride of life, is not of the Father, but is of the world." (1 John 2:15–16)

- "And when the woman saw that the tree was good for food, and that it was pleasant to the eyes, and a tree to be desired to make one wise, she took of the fruit thereof." (Genesis 2:6)

- "Either make the tree good; or else make the tree corrupt, and his fruit corrupt: for the tree is known by his fruit." (Matthew 12:32–34)

## 5. Who Was Responsible?

*Perfect Adam* Man is responsible. God cannot tempt man. Supporting verses:

". . . God cannot be tempted with evil, neither tempteth he any man." (James 1:13)

*Poor Adam* God was responsible. He placed Adam in a garden, right alongside of a tree filled with mouth-watering "fruit" that He told Him not to eat. As if the command (designed to produce *disobedience*) were not enough, He sent Satan into the garden to tempt Adam. And he did all of this *before* Adam had eaten from the fruit of the tree of the knowledge of good and evil, when Adam did *not yet know good and evil*. How was he supposed to make an informed decision? It's obvious that God is going to great lengths to show us that He was *behind* Adam's sin, even as He goes to great lengths to show us that he's behind ALL sin:

- "He hath concluded all in disobedience . . ." (Romans 11:32)

- "The creation was subjected to vanity . . ." (Romans 8:20)

- "I form the light, and create darkness: I make peace, and create evil: I the LORD do all these things." (Isaiah 45:7)

- "By his spirit he hath garnished the heavens; his hand hath formed the crooked serpent." (Job 26:13)

- Supporting verses:

- "For God hath concluded them all in unbelief . . ." (Romans 11:32)

- "The creature was made subject to vanity . . ." (Romans 8:12)

- "I form the light, and create darkness: I make peace, and create evil: I the LORD do all these things." (Isaiah 45:7)

- "By his spirit he hath garnished the heavens; his hand hath formed the crooked serpent." (Job 26:13)

## 6. How Will God Make It Right?

*Perfect Adam* There's nothing to make right. Man's sin is man's responsibility and man's problem. God will, however, redeem those members of Adam's race who accept Jesus Christ as their savior, thus assuring that the fall of Adam was not in vain. Supporting verses:

- ". . . whomsoever shall call upon the name of the Lord shall be saved." (Acts 2:21)

*Poor Adam* God will make it right by reconciling all to Himself (Eph. 1:10), becoming all in all (1 Cor. 15:28), and making all alive in Christ (1 Cor. 15:22).

Supporting verses:

- "That in the dispensation of the fullness of times he might gather together in one all things in Christ, both which are in heaven, and which are on earth . . ." (Ephesians 1:10)

- "And when all things shall be subdued unto him, then shall the Son also himself be subject unto him that put all things under him, that God may be all in all." (1 Cor. 15:28)

- "As in Adam all die, so in Christ will all be made alive." (1 Cor. 15:22)

The following table sums up the difference in the two views.

|  | Perfect Adam | Poor Adam |
|---|---|---|
| **How was Adam created?** | Adam was a perfect, immortal spiritual being. | Adam was created liable to sin and dissolution. |
| **Why was Adam created?** | In order to live forever in peace and harmony with Eve and the animals. | Presumably, there was a higher purpose. This purpose, it would appear, includes pain and suffering as a remedial discipline. |
| **Why did Adam fall?** | Perfect man decided he wanted to be like God. | Out of those liabilities inherent in his nature. |
| **How could a perfect man have fallen?** | He was perfect; it's a mystery how he fell into sin. | He couldn't; Adam wasn't perfect. |
| **Who was responsible?** | The creature. | The Creator, of course. |
| **How will it be rectified?** | God will make it right for some; He will eternally torment the rest. | God will make it right for us in the end; after all it would be unjust to give us a life—unasked for—that turned out to be a curse. |

# Job and Adam

Stephen King once described the book of Job as a Superbowl between God and Satan with Job as the human astroturf. Just before the opening kick-off we read in Job 1:12: "And the Lord said unto Satan, Behold, all that he hath is in thy power . . ." There you have it. In black and white. All that Job had was given over to *Satan's* power. God was not afflicting Job; Satan was afflicting Job.

Not so fast. Job 2:3: ". . . and still he holdeth fast to his integrity, although thou movest *me* against him . . ." Did Satan move *God*? Whose idea was this in the first place? "Now there was a day when the sons of God came to present themselves before the Lord, and Satan also came among them. And the Lord said unto Satan, Whence comest thou? Then Satan answered the Lord, and said, From going to and fro in the earth, and from walking up and down in it. And the Lord said unto Satan, Hast thou considered my servant Job . . ." (Job 1:6–8)? God initiated the entire proceeding. Satan was just his tool. Preston Eby writes:

> "We would now draw your reverent attention to the magnificent words which reveal Job's reaction to all this. "Then said his wife unto him, Do you still retain your integrity? Curse God and die!

But he said unto her . . . "What? Shall we receive good at the *hand of God* and . . . not receive evil. *In all this Job did not sin with his lips.*" (Job 2:9–10) Notice! Job never did recognize any such person as Satan in all his trouble. He recognized *only God* in this. . . . It will be an appalling shock to many precious people to learn that in *all* this Job did *not sin* with his lips! We have every right to conclude from this that Job was speaking the absolute truth when he attributed all of this evil to God. What he had said was right in the sight of God. No place did the Lord rebuke Job for his words in any way. In fact, in the end of the experience God said that Job had spoken *rightly* of Him and *all others had not.*"[8]

It seems that God uses Satan as a middle man, sometimes leaving us with the impression that there's a conflict between God's will and Satan's actions. There is not. To be sure, there is a conflict between Satan's *will* and God's will, but not between Satan's *actions* and God's will. What Satan desires for our detriment God desires for our good, and so He uses Satan to help accomplish His plans. The presence of this middle man leads to confusion about whose will is really being done and why. In a passage like the one above, however, God removes the middle man, and shows us whose will was really being done.

One would have to be blind not to see the parallel to the story of Adam and Eve. God was using Satan to accomplish *His* will. In the Job story He removes the middle man right there in the same book. Does He remove the middle man with regard to the Adam story? Yes, but not in the same book or even the same testament. He removes it in Romans 8:20–21: "For the creature was made subject to vanity, not willingly, but by reason of Him who hath subjected the same, in hope, Because the creature itself also shall delivered from the bondage of corruption into the glorious liberty of the children of God." Jim Strahan writes:

> "In Job . . . we have the story of an innocent man who lost [everything]. His . . . friends came to . . . help him make sense of the terrible circumstances. The discussions turned ugly when they told him that he was the cause of the evil. . . . What was not understood was that God had allowed the events, just as He set up the circumstances for Adam and Eve. . . . Job's friends concluded that Job's actions . . . were the causes, and goodness, evil, pain, and suffering were the effects. God's answer to Job was that He was the creator-cause, and goodness, evil, pain, and suffering are

8. Eby, "Two Hands of God."

part of the processes where . . . restoration . . . will be the effects. At the end . . . listen to the words of Job after experiencing the full brunt of evil." I know you can do everything and that no purpose of yours can be withheld. . . . I have uttered what I did not under-stand (why all this evil?). . . . I have heard of you . . . but now my eyes see You (as a result of this experience) therefore . . . I repent."[9]

## Was Sin Necessary?

Most Universalists and many Calvinists agree that sin was an integral part of God's plan for mankind. The Calvinists argue that God decreed sin for the purpose of demonstrating His justice by punishing it forever, whereas the Universalist insists that God decreed sin for a limited time and for educational purposes. The following quote by Theodore of Mopsuestia will suffice to sum up the Universalist viewpoint:

"God knew that men would sin in all ways, but permitted this result to come to pass, knowing that it would ultimately be for their advantage. For since God created man when he did not ex-ist, and made him ruler of so extended a system, and offered so great blessings for his enjoyment, it was impossible that He should have not prevented the entrance of sin if He had not known that it would be ultimately for his advantage. Therefore God divided the creation into two states, the present and the future. In the latter He will bring all to immortality and immutability. In the former He gives us over to death and mutability. For if He had made us at first immortal and immutable, we should not have differed from irra-tional animals, who do not understand the peculiar characteristics by which they are distinguished. For if we had been ignorant of mutability we could not have understood the good of immutabil-ity. Ignorant of death, we could not have known the true worth of immortality. Ignorant of corruption, we could not have properly valued incorruption. Ignorant of the burden of sinful passions, we could not have duly exulted in freedom from such passions. In a word, ignorant of an experiment of evils, we should not have been able properly to understand the opposite forms of good."[10]

9. Strahan and Meeker, "Who's in Charge?"

10 Taken from *A Dictionary of Christian Biography.*

Against this idea it has been argued that sin could not have been necessary for our development; if it were so, then what about the angels? Indeed what about God? Did they have to sin? Charles Pridgeon writes:

> "There are those who hold that there was a necessity of evil's entering for the developing and perfecting of free moral agents, that unless there is such a contest there would be no developing of strength. If evil is absolutely necessary, then evil must have had an eternal beginning; and evil would be necessary in God, so that He could be His best and His unfallen creatures become their very best. . . . If it had been necessary to sin in order to reach the highest moral and spiritual development, then the Lord Jesus Christ would of necessity have had to sin. The highest development of humanity is found in the Lord Jesus Christ when He was made man. Likewise, if sin were necessary for the highest development, all the angels who have never fallen, ought to fall in order to attain perfection. In these two cases we certainly see that sin was not a necessity for the perfection of the creature, nor was it God's highest plan."[11]

This answer fails to consider the nature of sin. Sin is rebellion against God; God would have no conceivable reason to rebel against Himself. The *battle* with sin, however, was necessary, or at least, it would seem, desirable.

But more about that later. First, it should be noted that just because sin wasn't necessary doesn't mean that it wasn't *inevitable* in the case of mortal creatures. Sin is not a necessary component of God's creation, but then neither is *man*. I would argue that the creation of man, coupled with the decision to leave him to his own devises, does render sin—if not necessary—than certainly inevitable. And when it comes to Omniscience we cannot separate inevitability from necessity. That which God renders inevitable is necessarily the best course of action and thereby necessary.

With regard to angels, they are *not* sons of God—at least not in the same sense as man. The angels are of a lower order than redeemed man; indeed they serve as "ministering spirits" (Heb. 1:14) to man, and, as such, they need not be conformed to the likeness of Christ in the *same manner* that we do. Man was made *lower* than the angels in order to one day be *higher* than them (Ps. 8:5, Luke 20:34–36). Does this not necessitate a form of discipline—evil, if you will—that the angels need never experience? Thomas Allin writes:

11. Pridgeon, *Is Hell Eternal? Or Will God's Plan Fail?* 61.

"A further consideration remains. As creation is for the Deity to enter into finite relations, and to subject His plans to definite limits, so, perhaps, evil, physical and moral, is in a sense inevitable. And it may be that, by the training and collision, thus involved, a higher type of character is formed than would be otherwise possible, e.g., self sacrifice, self restraint, sympathy, mercy, etc., seem to require a background of evil for their existence; although I believe that certain results of this have not always been thought out by its advocates. A creation thus advancing to perfection by a certain, if slow, victory over evil, may possibly be a nobler thing than a creation so safeguarded as to have never fallen."[12]

As for those angels that never fell, I would point to 1 Tim. 5:21, which mentions elect angels. For all we know, the elect angels were the ones God *kept* from falling. Given the chance, they might all have fallen.

With regard to Christ, it should be noted that He became God's only begotten son only after defeating sin (Heb. 5:5). Sin was a necessary—or at least a desirable—enemy in God's overall plan. Just as man needed something to overcome to attain fullness, so did Christ. Christ learned obedience by the things He suffered (Heb. 5:8). Of course one could argue, as Pridgeon does, that suffering is possible without sin. It can come in the form of resistance to sin. But for sin to be resisted it must first be given an opportunity. God must create enough distance between Himself and the creature to allow for the possibility of sin. This means at least some form of temptation must exist. This also means that some separation—at some point—is desirable and even necessary for moral progress. Of course Christ was able to resist *His* temptation. But could the *first* Adam be expected to perform as well?

"The first man is of the earth, earthy; the second man is the Lord from heaven." (1 Cor. 15:47)

The following verses make it plain that sin was inevitable—and therefore necessary—in the case of man.

"The first man Adam was made a living soul; the last Adam was made a quickening spirit." (1 Cor. 15:45)

"Now this I say, brethren, that flesh and blood cannot inherit the kingdom of God; neither doth corruption inherit incorruption." (1 Cor. 15:50)

12. Allin, *Christ Triumphant* ch 10.

"It is sown in corruption; it is raised in incorruption." (1 Cor. 15: 42)

"That which is born of the flesh is flesh; and that which is born of the Spirit is spirit." (John 3:6)

"They that are in the flesh cannot please God." (Romans 8:8)

It is evident that sin was in fact part of God's plan—not in a provisional sense, but as something that had to come to pass. If God had wanted Adam to successfully *resist* sin, then He would have made it happen by exactly the same methods he now employs to help Adam (mankind) *overcome* sin.

We have covered Pridgeon's argument with regard to the Father, the Son, the angels, and man. Similar reasoning applies to the Holy Spirit. The Holy Spirit played a vital role in the defeat of sin, and that defeat of sin added something to the stature of Christ; thus the entire godhead is glorified in the defeat of sin in a way it would otherwise not have been. Sin provided for an expression, a demonstration, a completeness, a victory that would not have been possible without it. Pridgeon's own words actually seem to *support* this idea:

> "In respect to the great mystery of the God-man we have always felt it to be a difficulty to accept the usual doctrinal statement that He was not man until He "was made flesh, and dwelt among us" and that ever after He had the indissoluble personality as the God-Man. It seemed to us as if the Godhead, in the Person of the Only Begotten Son, added something that it did not have before, and, as a consequence, was not absolutely complete in the past."[13]

What exactly was added if not Christ's victory over sin and the sons He gathered into Himself in the process? How could this have happened had sin never existed?

In any case, if there's something of a mystery as to why sin is needed in God's creation, it's a monumentally smaller mystery than the one entailed in the idea of evil springing from perfection.

## Are We the Garden?

As already noted, there are many versions of the Adam and Eve story and no two are exactly alike. I read a rather amazing interpretation online that

13. Pridgeon, *Is Hell Eternal? Or Will God's Plan Fail?* 83.

I believe has a great deal of merit. It's by an author by the name of Jacob Israel. I would like to share it here. Then we will move on—I promise!

According to this interpretation, the entire Adam and Eve story is a parable. The main points are as follows:

The garden of Eden is not a place. *We* are the garden!

The two trees—a tree of life and a tree of knowledge—are inside of *us*.

The Tree of Life is Christ.

The Tree of "knowledge" is our body, or carnal nature.

The tempting reptile is our brain.

Man prefers the fruit of the carnal tree. We rely on our senses and cater to our carnal nature.

Eating from this tree caused Christ to die inside of us.

When Christ died in us, we were separated from our true selves—expelled from the garden

The way back to the garden is guarded by cherubims

Cherubim means "imaginary creatures." Our false thoughts keep us from re-entering the garden

That's the general picture that Israel paints. The devil, however, is in the details—literally in this case! Let's take a look at them.

We begin with a question: Who are we? Colossians 3:4 says: "When Christ, who is our life, shall appear, then shall ye also appear . . ." Christ is who we truly *are*. But is that how we live? More to the point: Is that *where* we live? In other words, are we living *inside* ourselves? Preston Eby writes:

"Nothing is more evident in the Word of God than the fact that man had his beginning *in God* . . .' In the beginning *was* the Word, and the Word *was* with God, and the Word *was* God. In Him *was* life; and the life *was* the light of men" (Jn. 1:14). W-a-s! It is a wonderful fact that in Him *is* life, and His life *is* the light of every man who believes . . . It was into this realm *outside of Christ* . . . that Adam was banished when he partook of that strange tree of the knowledge of good and evil . . ."[14]

Where and how did this banishment occur? John 19:41 says "Now in the place where he was crucified there was a garden; and in this garden a

14. Eby, "The Law of Circularity."

new sepulchre." Christ was crucified at Golgatha—the place of the skull. He was killed *within us*—in our *minds*.

Read it again: "Now in the place where he was crucified there was a garden; and in this garden a new sepulchre."

Translation: "In the place where our TRUE LIFE was put to death there was a BODY, and in this BODY a tomb."[15] Christ died in us. Our spirit is dead. But our body is still there—quite alive and quite destructive. And in this body a tomb. There is death in this body. But Christ Himself is also in this dead body—in a tomb. Christ is *buried* in us. He died in us, He's buried in us, and He is waiting to rise again in us.

This is where the story gets *really* interesting. We are the garden. Two trees exist in us—Christ and our carnal nature. What is the tree that sits in the middle of us? It's the nervous system! It even looks like a tree. Israel provides the following description:

> "*Anatomy of the nevous system*: If you think of the brain as a central computer that controls all bodily functions, then the nervous system is like a network that relays messages back and forth from the brain to different parts of the body." He then goes on to note that "Christ . . . died the *instant mankind's soul* followed after the *snake hanging* on the *tree (nervous system)* in the middle . . . There is *literally* a snake hanging from that tree (the nervous system). It is called the *reptilian brain* ."

He then provides the following details from a scientific publication: *The Reptilian Brain/Complex*:

> "The R-complex consists of the brain stem and the cerebellum . . . Because the reptilian brain is primarily concerned with physical survival, the behaviors it governs have much in common with the survival behaviors of animals . . . The overriding characteristics of R-complex behaviors are that they are automatic, have a ritualistic quality, and are highly resistant to change."[16]

Why is it so hard to re-enter the garden? Genesis 3:24: "So he drove out the man; and he placed at the east of the garden of Eden cheribums, and a flaming sword which turned every way, to keep the way of the tree of life." Israel writes "The *translation* for *cheribum* is *imaginary creature*. The

---

15  This sentence was a direct quote from: Jacob Israel, "Garden of Eden Revealed."
16.  Israel, "Garden of Eden Revealed."

cheribum is *who we think we are*. It is our *carnal ego* that keeps us *living outside the garden* (us) instead of *within* (where God and Christ sit)."[17]

What's truly astonishing is how perfectly this theory accords with traditional Christian doctrine. Simply compare it with this excerpt from Shirley Guthrie's classic work entitled—what else?—*Christian Doctrine*.

> "Just when we are driven finally to biblical statements about Satan, we are driven to the conclusion that there *is* no explanation for the origin and reality of evil in God's world. The Genesis story is very profound in its simplicity at this point. It makes no attempt to explain where the Tempter came from or how he could exist at all in God's world. Satan is a hideous intruder who does not belong in the picture but is nevertheless there. Logically, evil is impossible in a world created and ruled by God, for it is just what God did *not* create and does *not* will. That is the parasitical power of evil. It is not the truth about what we are and what the world is like; it is a *lie*, a *contradiction* and *denial* of the truth."[18]

In other words, it is life outside of the garden.

---

17. Ibid .

18. Guthrie, *Christian Doctrine: Revised Edition* 182.

# 7

---

# Sin: Transfused or Imputed?

HEBREWS 2:14–15 SAYS: "FORASMUCH then are the children partakers of flesh and blood, he also himself likewise took part of the same; that through death he might destroy him that had the power of death, that is, the devil; And deliver them who through fear of death were all their lifetime subject to bondage."

This verse always struck a nerve with me. It seemed to be saying something important. It seemed to be conveying a message that I *wanted* to find in the bible, but couldn't. It seemed to be saying that we sin because we die. This verse gave me a ray of hope that maybe, just maybe, God understood that we mortals sin because of our frail, weak condition. If only the rest of the bible supported this idea. I knew, however, that it did not. All of the other verses were clear: we die because we sin. It's all our fault. One verse that *seemed* to say otherwise was not enough to overturn the clear teaching of the rest of scripture.

But is that the only verse? Or are there other verses that teach the same thing—verses that I had been conditioned to either ignore or to interpret with a certain bias? The question is: Do we die because we sin, or do we sin because we die? We begin with the cornerstone on which the doctrine of original sin is built—Romans 5:12. "Therefore, just as through one man sin entered into the world, and death through sin, and so death spread to all men, because all sinned . . ."

Tradition tells us that this verse is teaching that we die because we sinned in Adam. That's because it says "death spread to all men, *because* all sinned." Is that what this verse is saying? Let's suppose that it is. Let's look at the implications of such an interpretation. Death spread to all because all sinned.

Sin = death. No sin = no death.

Verse 13 goes on to say "For until the law sin was in the world: but sin is not imputed where there is no law." Where there's law, there's sin. Where there's sin, there's death.

Law = sin = death.

Where there's no law, there's no sin. Where there's no sin, there's no death.

No law = no sin = no death.

From Adam to Moses there was no law. Remember: No law = no sin = no death.

"*Nevertheless* death reigned from Adam until Moses . . ." (Rom. 5:14) What? Why is Paul contradicting himself? First he says that sin = death. Then he says that where there was *no sin* there was *still death*. From Adam to Moses there was no law and therefore *no sin*. Law = sin. No law = no sin. *Nevertheless* death reigned. What is he trying to say? It would seem that he's saying that even when there was no sin, there was still death. In other words, even people who were not sinning—as far as the law was concerned—were still dying. Why? If they were not dying because of their sin, then why were they dying? Go back to the Romans 5:12. "Therefore, just as through one man sin entered into the world, and death through sin, and so death spread to all men . . ." They were dying because *Adam* sinned. Take out the last part of that verse—because all sinned—and the rest of the passage makes perfect sense (although it was still a strange way to make the point if you ask me). But put that last phrase in and suddenly the passage seems very strange and cryptic. Could it be that there's a problem with that last phrase?

The problem is with the word *because*. In *Creation's Jubilee*, Stephen E. Jones takes up the issue.

> ". . . The translators would have us believe that death (mortality) spreads to all men *because* we sin . . . We can point to millions of abortions to prove that babies are mortal *before* they sin . . .
>
> Romans 5:12 says specifically that Adam's sin was imputed to all men, and as a direct result, "*death spread to all men.*" Paul repeats this concept in 1 Cor. 15:22, "*For as in Adam all die.*" . . .
>
> God . . . *imputed* his sin to our accounts. This would be a gross injustice . . . except for the fact that Jesus came to impute His righteousness to our accounts as well . . . This is also Paul's conclusion in Romans 5:18: "So then as through one transgression

there resulted condemnation to all men, even so through one act of righteousness there resulted justification of life to all men." Our liability for Adam's sin simply makes us mortal in this age. And that mortality . . . makes us morally weak . . . When Jerome translated the Latin Vulgate around 400 A.D., he rendered the last phrase of Romans 5:12, "*because we all sinned.*" . . . The Greek word used is *eph' ho. Eph'* or *epi*, means "on, upon, or over." The Greek word, *Ho*, means "which." The phrase "on which" or "over which" denotes a consequence or result to follow. To illustrate this, let us say, "I walked into a stumbling block, *on which* I fell." Did my fall cause the stumbling block to exist? Of course not . . . Yet the New American Standard version would have us render this: "I walked into a stumbling block, *because* I fell." . . . Church leaders . . . concluded that man received a sinful soul from Adam, rather than mortality . . . The truth is this: When Adam fell, his sin was *imputed* to us, *not* infused . . . When Adam's sin was imputed to us, God called us *all* sinners . . . The penalty was death . . . Therefore, also, in dealing with our salvation, Christ's righteousness was also imputed to us . . ."[1]

The mistranslation, Jones believes, was due to a confusion of the two deaths spoken of in the bible—the first and second death. He says that the translators, relying on verses like Romans 6:23 and 5:21, where sin causes death, "concluded that Paul must have made a mistake by saying that death was the cause of sin." In other words, Paul was talking about the first death, not the second. He goes on to state "There are two sins and two deaths spoken of in the Bible. The penalty for Adam's sin is the first death; God's judgment, lawful correction, and discipline for our own sins is the second death." Adam's sin, he asserts, is judged by means of the first death; our individual sins by means of the second.

Of course none of this is to say—and I don't think Jones would say it—that sin does not cause death. I believe Paul clearly taught that it does. But I don't believe he was teaching that our own personal sin is the reason we physically die. In other words, we *are* born dying for Adam's sin. And this condition *does* cause us to sin. But even so, sin causes death. Is that a contradiction? I don't think so. Even a person who knows nothing of scripture can see from experience that sin causes death. It doesn't mean he believes that he is personally responsible for his own mortality. But he still knows that drinking, smoking, doing drugs, and other such things, cause

---

1. Jones, "Creation's Jubilee."

death from both a physical and a spiritual perspective. I think Paul was less interested in how sin and death came about than in what to do about it. He meets us where we are. We are in this mess. We have been subjected to mortality, to a condition that creates sin. What now? For Paul there were two answers: continue in Adam's death or escape into Christ's life.

But I also believe he set forth the principle in Rom. 5:12 that God subjected us to death for *someone else's* sins. And although Paul doesn't touch on it, this act on God's part was a violation of His own laws (Deut. 24:16, Ezek. 18:20). I believe, therefore, that Paul, while teaching that sin causes death, *also* taught that death causes sin (Heb. 2:15) and that God would ultimately rescue man from the condition that *He* Himself imposed on them.

There's a dichotomy to Paul's writings: on the one hand, he places the onus for sin on man, and charges him with the responsibility for his own eternal destiny, and on the other, He places the responsibility on God, making clear that He subjected us to death and will one day get us out. In other words, he treats both the relative (man) and the absolute (God), both the proximate cause (man) and the root cause (God). Man is the proximate— or nearest cause—of his own sin. He sins because he wants to sin. Such a path can only lead to eternal destruction. On the other hand, there's a root cause for sin. The failure to discern between the root and absolute is why the traditional interpretation of Rom 5:12 has prevailed: it seems to make man both the proximate *and* root cause of sin, which seems to accord better with much of Paul's writings. It certainly accords better with the idea of eternal torment. It is clear, however, in many other verses that Paul *does* acknowledge God as the root cause.

The real issue is this: Does Rom 5:12 establish a *foundation* whereby man is both the root and proximate cause of sin, thereby justifying God should he choose to forever damn most of humanity? Or does it establish a *foundation* whereby man is the proximate cause of sin and God the root cause, thereby creating for God an obligation to vindicate His justice by saving all men?

Which option we choose will color how we understand the rest of the chapter. Rom. 5:15 says: "But not as the offense, so also is the free gift. For if through the offense of one many be dead, much more the grace of God, and the gift by grace, which is by one man, Jesus Christ, hath abounded unto the many." The following excerpt from a debate between Tom Talbott and Eric Landstrom represent the two different ways of understanding this verse.

Talbott: "Paul insists that the one, namely Adam, was a type of Jesus Christ (vs. 14), in that Jesus, the second Adam, stands in the same relationship to the many as the first Adam did. But with this difference: if the many died by the trespass of the one man, how much more did God's grace and the gift that came by the grace of the one man, Jesus Christ, overflow to the many."

Landstrom: "For if one man's offense meant that men should be slaves to death all their lives; it is a far greater thing through another Man, Jesus Christ offers salvation to all men. Men by their acceptance of His more than sufficient grace and righteousness should live their lives as kings knowing that their salvation is assured. There is no comparison between the sin of Adam and the grace of God. The free gift of grace covers all sins, not just Adam's offense. Verse 15 is just saying that when measured by time, the victory of Christ is far greater than Adam's sin. Because Adam's sin is only temporary, whereas Jesus Christ's victory is forever! This verse does not say all are saved!"[2]

It might surprise the reader to hear that I believe Landstrom's interpretation is the correct one. How can I side with Landstrom and still argue for Universalism? Remember, our understanding of Romans 5:12 will color our understanding of other verses. I believe that Romans 5:12 establishes a *foundation* whereby man is the proximate cause of sin and God the root cause, thereby creating for God an obligation to vindicate His justice by saving all men. The injustice will be rectified in stages, over a great deal of time and many generations. Romans 5:15 is *not* addressing the ultimate outcome, only the *power* of the remedy provided for those *now appropriating it.* The emphasis is on the efficacy of Christ's grace, and its *immediate* scope, which includes, as Landstrom understands, those who appropriate that grace. The emphasis is not on the final scope of the remedy. Christ will take away the *sin* of the world (Jn 1:29). But in the meantime He is taking away the *sins* of the world (1 Jn 2:2). It is this latter phase that Paul is concerned with. Paul's letter addresses itself to the relative and the immediate, but intimates that there is a long-term, absolute victory in view. He clearly establishes that all died in Adam (apart from any act of will on their part), then *seems* to suggest that *some* will be made alive in Christ (contingent upon their acceptance of His grace). There is a glaring judicial tension there that demands a resolution. The resolution is intimated at in Rom 5:18, which, unlike Rom. 5:15, seems to place the emphasis not on the

2 Online debate between Tom Talbott and Eric Landstrom.

*power* of Christ's grace, but on its scope, drawing what appears to be a clear parallel between the scope of Adam's sin and the scope of Christ's grace. It says: "Therefore as by the offense of one judgment came upon all men to condemnation; even so by the righteousness of one the free gift came upon all men unto justification of life."

I believe the fact that traditional teaching has opted for the first of the two foundational understandings of Rom. 5:12 (man is root cause and effect) has colored the way we look at the verses that seem to teach the second (God is root cause; man is proximate cause).

8

# The Penalty for Sin

WE HAVE MADE OUR way through the first two sets of opposing doctrines that flow naturally from our two opposing starting points, namely, the Calvinist starting point, whereby God is not the Universal Father, and the Universalist starting point, whereby He is. The next doctrine is that of the Atonement. What did Christ suffer on the cross? For whom? And why did He have to suffer it? These questions have been debated for centuries, and I will not pretend to have a perfect answer to them. In fact, I will limit myself to trying to prove just three things: First, that the Calvinist model of the Atonement contradicts their own theology, secondly, that an alternative understanding of the Atonement is possible, and thirdly, that the traditional model does not really allow that *anyone's* sins can be paid for. I shall go no farther than this.

## Calvinist Model of Atonement at Odds with Their Own Theology

The Calvinists generally operate on the substitutionary atonement model, whereby Christ serves as a sacrifice or propitiation for sin. According to this model, God, in order to be able to forgive sin, requires that his wrath be appeased. He is so angry at the sinner that He cannot forgive him unless a payment is made. This payment is made in the form of Christ, who takes on the sin of the world, and is then punished for that sin. This allows the Father to now offer forgiveness. A Calvinist might differ with me on a detail or two here, but I think I have painted a essentially accurate portrait of their position. This position, however, is at odds with their own theology.

There are two reasons, as far as I can tell, as to why God might get angry over our sins. The first reason is found in Proverbs 14:31 and 17:5. God identifies sin against man as sin against God. In other words, if I hurt you it offends God. He takes it personally, as if I had hurt Him. But it's hard to imagine that this could serve as the grounds for God's anger according to Calvinist theology, which insists that God does not identify with man in this manner; in fact he hates most men. Sin against them shouldn't bother Him at all. If it does bother Him, it is only because it represents disobedience to *Him*. But why should that make Him angry? Disobedience, or sin, is merely a necessary step in God's plan to punish man for all eternity. Why would God be angry at man for doing what He created him to do? Does anybody in the known universe ever get angry at an occurrence which they desire and bring about in order to facilitate a goal which they themselves have set? It is this type of convoluted logic that leads us to what I call the Calvinist *Happy Coincidence* model of sin and salvation. It goes like this:

1. From eternity past God intended that the most vivid and profound demonstration of his glory would come in the form of his work of salvation on the cross of Christ.

2. God then made man to punish him

3. He made him perfect and thus unlikely to ever need punishing, or, for that matter, a savior

4. By a happy coincidence, and against all the odds, this perfect man sinned, thus allowing God to fulfill His purposes for both the man and Christ

5. When he sinned, God, who is suddenly confronted with the prospect of being able to fulfill all of His original plans, becomes *furious*

It is this inexplicable fury, grounded in absolutely nothing, that forms the basis for the Calvinist idea of the atonement. It ought to be rejected by anyone of sound mind.

## An Alternate Model of the Atonement

This brings me to the second of the three stated aims of this chapter, which is to offer a different model for the atonement, one where Christ went to the cross, not in order to endure punishment in our stead, but to heal us of sin.

In fairness to traditionalists, verses that speak of "Christ bearing our griefs" or "bearing our sins in his body" seem to argue decisively for a substitutionary atonement theory. But are they as decisive as they seem? Let's look at three three such verses:

"Surely he hath borne our griefs, and carried our sorrows: yet we did esteem him stricken, smitten of God, and afflicted. But he was wounded for our transgressions, he was bruised for our iniquities: the chastisement of our peace was upon him; and with his stripes we are healed." (Isaiah 52:4–5)

"Who his own self bare our sins in his own body on the tree, that we, being dead to sins, should live unto righteousness: by whose stripes ye were healed." (1 Peter 2:24)

"And he cast out the spirits with his word, and he healed all that were sick; that it might be fulfilled what was spoken by Esaias the prophet, saying, "Himself took our infirmities and bare our sicknesses." (Matthew 8:16–17)

Of these three verses, Thomas Thayer writes:

"Matthew 8:16,17, is a perfect commentary on Isaiah and Peter." And he cast out the spirits with his word, and he healed all that were sick; that it might be fulfilled which he spoke by Esaias the prophet, saying, "Himself took our infirmities and bare our sicknesses." Now, in what sense did, or could, Jesus take the infirmities of those who were diseased, or bear their sicknesses? What did he do in their case? We are told in the preceding words: "He *healed* all that were sick." This is the equivalent of the phrase, "he bare our sicknesses;" which, in a physical sense, is the equivalent of the phrase, "he bare our sins," in a moral sense."[1]

## Traditional Model Means that Nobody Can Be Saved

If the penalty for sin is eternal torment, then it remains unpaid for all of humanity. The obvious argument against the notion that Christ suffered

1. Thayer, *Theology of Universalism*, 144.

eternal torment is the fact that the only equivalent to an eternity in hell *is* an eternity in hell. Christ is not still in hell. Consequently, He did not pay for anyone's sins and indeed never could.

The only defense against this argument is that God, being infinite, was able to endure eternal torment and come out the other end. I believe this argument is flawed. Yes, it is true that God probably exists outside of time. Eternal torment, however, does not. It's very nature is bound up in time; indeed the essence of eternal torment is unending *duration*. Duration requires time. To experience eternal torment as man must experience it is to endure an unending duration of torment. If God's nature provides an escape clause that allows Him to experience eternal torment *followed* by eternal bliss, then He is not really enduring the same punishment as *we* would have to suffer, namely, eternal torment that is *not* followed by eternal bliss.

Let me use an illustration. Suppose two men commit an offense for which the penalty is a fine of one million dollars. This particular figure just so happens to equal the net worth of the first man, but it constitutes only a fraction of the net worth of the second. Are they both paying the same penalty in terms of an objective standard of justice? In terms of the damage exacted from them? Of course they are not. For the first man, the penalty is enough to destroy him. For the second, it is a mere pittance. Apparently eternal torment—whatever that is—is a blow delivered by God that Christ can endure and man cannot. But to be the same punishment, the blow has to be adjusted according to the size of its target. Imagine that we have two men that commit the same transgression. One man is of average size; the other is a hundred feet tall. Now, suppose that the figure dispensing the punishment is two hundred feet tall, and the punishment is this: One punch, delivered at maximum impact, to the tip of the chin. Now imagine he delivers this same exact punishment to both men. Has he *really* dispensed the same punishment to both? Of course he hasn't. In order to deliver the same punishment, the power of the punch would have to be adjusted according to each man's ability to endure it.

Moreover, if God's nature allows for an escape from hell, then why doesn't He confer that nature on man? One might argue that such a thing is impossible due to the fact that only God is infinite. But why can't God confer upon us any attribute He wishes? Isn't the whole argument for hell based on the idea that Adam was somehow infinite, and thereby capable of infinitely offending God? Why can't God transform His creatures in a way that enables them to endure the same punishment He did and then, like Him, come out the other side? Doesn't the argument for eternal torment include the idea that man will be given supernatural durability that he might be able to endure his punishment forever without expiring? Why is it that he can sin as if He were God, he can endure punishment as if he were God, but unlike God, he can never come out the other end? What a cruel irony that God made man just infinite enough to offend Him infinitely, but not infinite enough that he could, like God, come out the other end of eternal torment.

Moreover, if the penalty for sin really was eternal torment, then why would Christ have allowed sin into the world in the first place, knowing that He would have to endure such a punishment? I submit that if eternal torment really were the punishment, then Christ would not have paid it. An eternity of pain followed by an eternity of bliss is not such a good deal. It would mean Christ's life—on balance—was as bad as it was good.

But what about annihilation? The annihilationist scoffs at the idea that God endured eternal torment, only to replace it with an even greater absurdity—eternal death. It is even more impossible to imagine that Christ suffered eternal death than it is to imagine that He suffered eternal torment. At least you could imagine eternal torment being condensed into a finite period of time by virtue of an increase in the intensity. Such a conception, however, is impossible with eternal death. Christ is either blotted out of existence or He is not. We know that He is not; therefore it is obvious that He did not suffer annihilation, and therefore He did not pay for anyone's sins *if* the penalty for sin is *eternal* death. But the bible never says the penalty for sin is *eternal* death; nor does it say it is eternal torment. That leaves only one option left. Is it possible that the penalty—death—is commutable not just in Christ's case, but in the case of all who must suffer it? Just how long must God's wrath burn before it is quenched? And what comes after? The answer will largely depend on the antecedent vision of God we apply to certain concepts and phrases. Let's explore one of them now.

## Three Versions of Eternal Fire

Radio preacher Harold Camping used to be an avid fire and brimstone preacher. No-one more zealously consigned his fellow man to an eternity of torture than "Brother" Camping. Then, after formulating an exact date for the end of the world, which produced certain changes in his eschatological perspective, he became an Annihilationist. Suddenly, he began declaring that the doctrine of eternal torment made God into a monster. In defense of his new doctrine, he pointed to Jude 1:7, which, he said, gave us a definition of eternal fire.

> "Moreover, God in his wonderful kindness gives us an example of eternal fire. When Sodom was destroyed, that fire literally burned, at most, a few days. Yet the fire that destroyed Sodom and Gomorrah is spoken of as "eternal fire." Even as Sodom and Gomorrah, and the cities about them, in like manner giving themselves over to fornication, and going after strange flesh, are set forth for an example, suffering the vengeance of eternal fire." Therefore, we can be assured that for these reasons and other biblical reasons, we can know that the traditional view of eternal damnation is bankrupt . . ."[2]

But why did he stop there? Ezekiel tells us that Sodom and Gomorrah are to be restored (Ezek. 16:55). Why isn't eternal fire a symbol for a *corrective* judgment?

Let's look at the three views of eternal fire and the implications of each view as to the punishment Christ suffered on the cross. Let's see which view makes the most sense.

1. Eternal fire means eternal torment. On this view the penalty for sin is eternal torment. Christ suffered eternal torment, then came out the other side.

2. Eternal fire means annihilation. On this view the penalty for sin is eternal death. Christ suffered eternal death, then came out the other side.

3. Eternal fire means corrective punishment. On this view the penalty for sin is death. Christ died, was buried, and then resurrected. He now lives forevermore.

Which of the three penalties did Christ *really* suffer? We all know the answer to that question is number three. And isn't that what it all comes down to? Exactly what *is* the penalty for sin? If we are unsure, then we need only to look to the cross for our answer. The penalty, most assuredly, is not eternal torment, nor eternal death. If God demands this of any man, then He is demanding a greater penalty than the law allows and that Christ himself paid.

2. Camping, *To God Be The Glory!*, 5.

The same logic can be applied to the lake of fire. Either it's eternal torment, eternal death, or *corrective* punishment. The bible says to compare spiritual with spiritual. Can we find a spiritual match in scripture for the lake of fire? Let's see.

> Rev. 21:8–9, 15 "And [Satan] shall go out to deceive the *nations . . .* to *gather them together . . .* and fire came down from God out of heaven, and *devoured* them . . . And whomsoever was not found written in the book of life was cast into the lake of fire."

> Zeph. 3:8–9 "Therefore wait upon Me, says the Lord, until the day that I rise up to the prey: for My determination is to *gather the nations,* that I may assemble the kingdoms, to pour upon them Mine indignation, even all My fierce anger: for all the earth shall be *devoured with the fire of my jealousy.* For then will I turn to the people a pure language, that they may all call upon the name of the Lord, to serve Him with one consent." (Zeph. 3:8–9)

The eternal torment vs. annihilation debate is a curious thing. The eternal tormentors argue that God's holiness is in no way compromised by eternally tormenting his own creation. The Annihilationist tries to refute him by arguing that a "loving" God would never, ever, under any circumstances eternally torment his own creatures—He would just destroy them! Unfortunately, the vast majority of Christians have never even considered the third alternative. Annihilation is not the best we can hope for. As Rob Bell said, "the good news is better than that."[3]

---

3. Bell, *Love Wins,* 191.

# PART 3

God's Mercy Will Extend to All

# 9

## We Hold These Truths to Be Self Evident

As promised, we have explored the two opposing sets of doctrines that proceed from the opposing starting points of Calvinism and Universalism. The only doctrine left concerns the question of whether or not God's mercy extends to all. In the next two chapters I will argue that it does. First, I will set out to prove that Universalism is founded on self-evident truths and that we are entirely justified—and even obligated—to interpret scripture in light of those truths. Then I will explore the judgment verses of scripture and argue, in keeping with my premise, that they can be reasonably interpreted as pertaining to corrective punishment rather than eternal damnation.

I do not intend to mount a particularly rigorous defense of Universalism, per se. That's because I did not really write this book for that purpose. I have read many such books that make the case quite nicely—better than I could ever hope to. But in my readings I have noticed a certain phenomenon. Most Universalists argue almost as if Calvinists do not exist. For instance, they often cite God's absolute sovereignty over all things—including the human will—as strong evidence for the Universalist position. As a former Calvinist, however, I would often read such things and find myself thinking "But so what if God's will is always done? The question is: What *is* God's will?" Don't get me wrong; I'm not saying these authors do not make a compelling case. They certainly do. But for a Calvinist these arguments may only serve to beg the question: What *is* God's will? So what if His will is always done? Does that necessarily dictate a good end for all men? This is the very presumption that the Calvinist rejects. The Calvinist does not allow that it's more reasonable to believe that God wills a good end for all than a bad end for most. We must not, according to the Calvinists, allow that it is more likely that all "will be made alive in Christ" than it is that most will "be tormented forever and ever" in the lake of fire simply because it seems like the right thing for God to do. We must be neutral on that point and let the bible decide. And so with this book I set out to argue why such an attitude is wrong from a hermeneutic standpoint and impossible from a practical one. I am seeking to establish that we are obliged to begin our search for truth from a vantage point of what *ought to be*. I am seeking to prove that Universalism rests on truths that are *self-evident*, and that the opposition has not come close to meeting the burden of proof needed to overturn these truths. *That* is the main thrust of the book. That and to show how one doctrine leads to another and to deal with each one. I have completed the latter part; I wish to do more work on the former. With this chapter I hope to examine from a variety of angles the fact that the case for Universalism relies on truths which all men everywhere regard to be self-evident, and that it is only with regard to scripture that we try to deny these truths.

## Self Evident Truth One: If I Were Christ, I'd Be Like Him

Richard Oerton writes:

> "In our civilization now this really is the attitude which we bring to bear on criminals. Let this thought—if I were you, I'd be a better man than you are—marinate for a few moments. If we analyse it soberly, we can see that it's crazy. But we don't analyse it. We don't even express it in words. Yet we harbour it nonetheless: in fact, we harbour it all the more. If I were you, of course I shouldn't be better than you; I should be just the same as you, and I should behave just as you do."[1]

The statement I just quoted was not made by a great Christian theologian. In fact, as far as I can tell, the man who made it was not even a Christian. Or a theologian, for that matter. But I would like to suggest that the sentiment it embraces yields a harvest of knowledge and insight that tells us, in the simplest form possible, everything there is to know about the relationship between Christ and Adam and all of the implications that it holds for our past, present, and future. The simple fact is this: If Christ were

---

1. Oerton et al., *The Nonsense of Free Will*, ch 5.

me, he would have sinned, and if I were Christ, I would not have. A bold statement, perhaps, but one which, I believe, is fully supported by scripture, along with all of the implications that proceed from it. Moreover, I wish to suggest that this statement proves that sin was necessary, mitigates our guilt, and points to an ultimate resolution that will extend to all creation. From a philosophical perspective, this may seem intuitive and fair. After all, how can a fair God judge us by a standard that He, if He were us, could not have met? From a religious perspective, however, it may seem irreverent. And although you will sometimes hear this argument *inferred*, you will rarely hear it stated so bluntly. But I believe it is necessary to do so, for it goes to the very crux of the matter, and facing it squarely will help us cut through a great deal of the confusion, double-talk, and deliberate obfuscation surrounding this issue.

Now, here's the interesting part. This idea—that I, if I were you, would do exactly as you do—is already accepted as fact by the Christian religious system. Sadly, however, it has been employed not to mitigate guilt, but rather to *establish* it. In fact, the doctrine of original sin is actually *built* on this concept. "Wherefore, as by one man sin entered into the world, and death by sin; and so death passed upon all men, for that all have sinned . . ." (Romans 5:12)

The traditional interpretation of this verse is this: We all sinned in Adam; therefore we all deserve whatever punishment is incurred by the act of a perfect man sinning. When one objects "But I didn't commit that sin" he is met with the response "But, you, if you were Adam, *would* have committed it; hence God was justified in condemning you in Adam." This is *the* Christian doctrine from which all others flow.

But look at how hard Christians try to evade the implications of this doctrine. Adam, they insist, was a glorious spiritual being with perfect free will. Given his perfect nature and optimal environment, the odds of him sinning were exceedingly small. In other words, Adam's guilt stemmed from the fact that he might have done otherwise than what he did. But this model—which is supposed to establish guilt—actually does the reverse. If Adam might have acted differently, then how is he *more* guilty? He is *less* guilty. Adam's sin, according to this theory, did not flow out of his nature; it *contradicted* it. But since when does such a thing *increase* guilt? Does a judge hand out a harsher sentence when he thinks the offender acted in accordance with his nature or against it? Surely when he acts *in accordance*. Sinning against one's nature is a *mitigating* circumstance. It wasn't *the real me*! In order to establish guilt, there had to be a fixity to Adam's decision. It had to come from his nature. And it must be the case that he might not have done otherwise. Adam was not guilty because he might have acted differently; he was guilty because he might *not* have acted differently. Otherwise, the only thing he was guilty of was having a bad day. How could Adam's sin establish him and his whole race as inveterate sinners if God simply caught him in a bad moment? And how could it mean that you or me in his place would have *necessarily* done the same? On this model God's response would be tantamount to a boss catching a normally diligent employee slacking on the job and declaring him a bad employee.

The problem is that we look to Romans 5:12 only as a means of establishing guilt, but ignore the fact that it is employed as the first part of an equation designed to establish *innocence*. Our guilt had to be fixed in Adam not, as tradition teaches, in order that God might be just in punishing us, but that He might be just in *justifying* us. God had to bind us all in Adam's guilt in order to include us all in Christ's righteousness.

The formula is simple. It is in two parts. If I were Adam, I would have sinned:

> "Why, as by one man sin entered into the world, and death by sin; and so death passed on all men, for that all have sinned" (Romans 5:12).

And if I were Christ, I would not sin.

> "Therefore as by the offense of one judgment came on all men to condemnation; even so by the righteousness of one the free gift came upon all men to justification of life" (Romans 5:18).

The verses in between the two aforementioned verses make it clear that this binding of all in Adam came about by way of a pre-ordained plan. There was no element of chance in it; nor any whiff of contingency. We were all bound up by God in Adam's sin that we might be made free by Christ's righteousness. Our identity, our moral constitution, our character, was *fixed* in Adam that it might be equally fixed in Christ.

Adolf E. Knoch put it this way:

> Ultimate reconciliation was first in the heart of God. There never would have been any estrangement without it. Therefore enmity was introduced in a manner closely corresponding with the way it is overcome. Because salvation was planned to be the great achievement of the Son of God's love, the One to Whom creation

first came into being, therefore sin was planned to reach the race through the failure of the one in whom it was created. Adam's offense is an inverted silhouette, a shadowgraph reversed, of the sacrifice of Christ. In their main outlines, their outstanding features, they are alike, though as far apart as the poles in moral values.

We may suppose that sin could have been introduced in a different way. It might have been limited to Adam, and each of his progeny might have been tested as he was, so that it would have been an individual failure. Adam might have had a considerable progeny before his transgression, who would have been free from the effects of his offense. So the race might have been broken up into groups or units. But God did not arrange it so. Sin must enter through one man because it was to be settled through One. The relation between Adam and his descendants must correspond to that which existed between God's Son and creation. Both could act on behalf of all who had been in them.[2]

## Two Men; Two Temptations

And when the woman saw that the tree was good for food, and that it was pleasant to the eyes, and a tree to be desired to make one wise, she took of the fruit thereof, and did eat, and gave also unto her husband with her; and he did eat. (Genesis 3:6)

Then was Jesus led up of the Spirit into the wilderness to be tempted of the devil. And when he had fasted forty days and forty nights, he was afterward a hungered. And when the tempter came to him, he said, If thou be the Son of God, command that these stones become bread. But he answered and said, It is written, Man shall not live by bread alone, but by every word that proceedeth out of the mouth of God. (Matthew 4:1–4)

So why did Christ succeed where we failed? Is it because He's better than us? Well, yes. Of course He's better than us. But why is He better than us? Because He's God? Well, yes. Of course He's God, and of course God is better than us. But that's not really what I'm getting at. What I'm asking is this: Why did Christ, in the flesh, tired and weak, manage to succeed where man failed? The answer is simple. He was stronger than man. He had an unfair advantage. This is something that the Christian religious system has tried to deny. They have tried to level the playing field between Adam and Christ. They have employed two tactics to do this. First, they have foisted

2. Knoch et al., *All in All*, 39.

upon us the myth of a *spiritual* Adam in order to raise him to Christ's level. Secondly, they have downplayed the severity of Adam's temptation while exaggerating the severity of Christ's.

First, consider Adam's temptation. There are two ways of looking at it. The first—emphasized by the traditional church—is this: Adam was a perfect man living in an optimal environment, with full access to every manner of delight, except one. It is this one thing he stubbornly insisted on having.

The other way of looking at it is this: Adam is placed in a garden. Right smack dab in the middle of this garden God places a tree filled with the most delectable, succulent, juiciest fruit Adam has ever seen. Then, to make matters worse, he tells Adam he can eat of any other tree except that delicious looking one in the middle. Then, as the icing on the cake, He sends Satan into the garden to tempt Adam into eating the fruit of that tree. Now, let's be honest: Which of the two scenarios paints a truer picture of what Adam was really up against? Likewise, there are two ways of looking at Christ's temptation.

Christ, weak and tired, is promised a variety of wonderful delights, yet somehow manages to resist.

Or,

Christ, who is God almighty, filled with the Spirit, says no thanks to the devil's pathetic attempts to give him the kingdoms that are already His. Now, let's be honest: Which of the two scenarios paint a truer picture of what Christ was really up against?

The truth is that Adam's temptation was greater.

Adam, a *man*, was confronted with the possibility of becoming a *God*
Or,
continuing to live exactly as he was.
On the other hand, Christ, a *God*, could become a *sinner*
Or,
*for the joy set before him* he could endure the cross and be *seated at the right hand of the father* for the rest of eternity, where He would be glorified *with the glory which [He] had before the world was* (Heb. 12:2, John 17:5)

Christ was faced with infinite reward for a short span of suffering, whereas Adam faced no reward for a lifetime of self-denial.

But there were other reasons why Christ succeeded where Adam failed. Christ understood the nature of temptation better than Adam. Adam had never been tempted; he had not yet eaten from the fruit of the tree of the knowledge of good and evil. He was not as "wise as serpents" (Matthew 10:16). He was overmatched!

But perhaps the strongest reason was that Christ had a more intimate relationship with the Father than Adam ever had. At the time of his transgression, Adam was not saved. If he was, he could not have sinned (1 Jn. 3:9). He had no real relationship with the Father at all. He had a love for the world, but he lacked a very important ingredient that he *absolutely needed* to overcome this love. He lacked a *greater love* than his love for the world. He lacked the love for the Father that Christ had in super-abundance. Yes, Christ *may* have been tempted by the bread offered by Satan, but what is the response: "Man does not live by bread alone . . ." (Matthew 4:4). And what is Christ's bread? It is to "do the will of him that sent me" (Jn. 4:34). Christ had a *perfect* relationship of complete trust and absolute *dependence* with the Father. He did *nothing* of His own (John 5:30). His trust was absolute. Why? Because of the intimate personal relationship he had with God *before the world was* (John 17:5). Christ had passions. He was tempted as we are in all ways, yet without sin (Heb. 4:15). Why? The temptation was there. The physical body was there. What enabled him to resist where Adam couldn't? He had a stronger counterbalance. That counterbalance was the Father Himself. And this is how it always is with the will. We always, without exception, at all times, in all places, do what we *most want to do*. We follow our strongest impulse. God has not yet developed in mankind the *love that conquers fear* (1 Jn. 4:18). But in due time He will. And when he does, we, just as surely as Christ, and the Father himself, will *not be able to sin*. (1 Jn. 3:9, Heb. 6:18) We will be just like Christ.

A great deal of understanding becomes available when we see the picture for what it really is. Christ and Adam were not equals. Christ did not set out to *out-do* Adam in order to have a judicial basis for condemning him and his race; He is a superior who employed His superior abilities to do for man what he could not do for himself. This is apparent even from the most cursory glance at the Adam story. Set before him in the garden were two trees—a tree of life and a tree of the knowledge of good and evil. Adam chose the latter because he did not have the former—the *life*—in himself. Christ is the life. If Adam had this life in him, he could not have sinned (1 Jn 3:9). Christ did have this life. Yes, He was confronted with temptations. He was, in effect, tempted to eat of the "bad" tree. Why was He able to resist? The answer is very simple. Because he had already eaten—and was always eating—from the "good" tree—the tree of life. When tempted he replied

"Man does not live by bread alone, but by every word from the mouth of God" (Matthew 4:4). His "bread" was to "do the will of the one who sent me." He endured the cross for the "joy set before him" (Heb. 12:2). This is the same joy He had known "before the world was" (Jn. 17:5).

Why is temptation so hard to resist? There are two reasons. First, we imagine that there's nothing better than the thing that is tempting us. Secondly, we can't see ourselves resisting the temptation for the rest of our lives, so we might as well give in. But Christ had neither of those problems. Let me use an illustration. Suppose a man is an alcoholic. Staring up at him from the table is an mug of cold, frothy beer. What is this man likely to be thinking at this moment? He's probably thinking that nothing in the universe can be quite as wonderful as that beer. He's also likely to be wondering how he is going to resist that beer every single day for the rest of his life. And these two things are likely to make the temptation irresistible.

Now suppose it is Christ who is looking down into that cold, frothy beer. And let's just assume that He happens to extremely thirsty at that particular moment. In fact, he is parched. What is he likely to be thinking? Well, for one thing he knows without question that this beer is not the greatest thing in the universe. In fact, it is not even close. He has already personally experienced a myriad of delights that are a million times greater than those produced by the taste of beer. Moreover, He knows that after resisting this beer those delights are waiting for Him. He knows that in time—and not much time at that—He will get *what he most wants*.

"... who for the joy that was set before him endured the cross ..."

"And now, Oh Father, glorify me with thine own self with the glory which *I had before the world was*."

Would he have any trouble resisting the beer? Would a king on his way to a specially prepared feast have any trouble resisting a hot dog at a concession wagon? Of course not. And this fact sheds much light on that curious statement that insists that Christ cannot "be tempted with evil" (James 1:13). I used to wonder how, if Christ can't be tempted, *was* he tempted? The truth is that Satan did tempt Christ, but Christ was never tempted. The "temptation" probably had no more appeal to Him than the hot dog to that king on his way to the feast. The bottom line is this: Adam sinned because he was not in Christ. Christ resisted sin because He was *in* God. When man's creation is complete, however, and he is fully in the image of God, he will be just as much in Christ as Christ is in God, and at that time he will not be able to sin.

## A New Creation

God made Adam in his image. On this all Christians are in agreement. But what they fail to appreciate is the fact that the action is ongoing. God is *making* Adam—and by extension all mankind—in his image. Adam was the first of a two-part equation that is to constitute the *true* image of God. This should be obvious from a few simple observations. Who is the image of God? Christ, of course. Who and what is Christ? He is God. And He is man. He is the God-man. This means God, if He created man in His image, intended that man should also be a God-man. Was Adam a God-man? The traditional religious system has gone to great lengths to show that he was. But there is a very simple test which might be employed which will reveal the true answer. It is so simple that it's astounding that anyone has ever missed it.

There are two things that determine our conduct: nature and character. The first is inherited; the second must be developed. Matthew 12:32–34 tells us our character proceeds from our nature. Inherit a human nature and you will develop human character. This character will include sin. Inherit a divine nature and you will develop divine character. This character will not include sin. Man sins. God doesn't. This is how we know Adam was not yet a God-man. He sinned. 2 Cor. 5:17 tells us "if any man be in Christ, he is a new creation." What is this new creation? It is very simple. It is the old man (Adam) *plus* the new man (Christ). How is this new creation created? By the usual means of transmission of life. A seed. "We are born again not of corruptible seed, but incorruptible, through the living and abiding word of God" (1 Peter 1:23). And what is the result of this transmission of life? This new creation? A new nature—one that is capable of resisting sin. "Whoever is born of God doth not commit sin; for his seed remaineth in him; and he cannot sin . . ." (1 John 3:9) It is only this kind of man, this new creation, this God-man, that can resist sin. And he resists it not because of an act of will, but because of a new nature. He is born again "not of the will of man" (Jn. 1:13). A look at 1 Cor. 15 reveals nothing if not the fact that Adam and Christ were separate. The entire passage is stressing a division, a gap, a distance between the two. A bridge meant to be crossed *in time*. Let's take it verse by verse.

42 "So also is the resurrection of the dead. It is sown in corruption;
it is raised in incorruption . . ."

This states the matter quite clearly: God sowed us in corruption. We do not sow ourselves. God sows us. The traditional theology would have us read the verse this way: "It is sown in honor; it falls into corruption, then it is restored to perfection." But of course the verse says nothing of the sort, nor does it imply it in any way. Moreover, the following verses reinforce the meaning.

43 "It is sown in dishonour; it is raised in glory: it is sown in weakness; it is raised in power."

Once again, we have the very same meaning and intent. God sowed us in weakness. It did not come as the result of The Fall.

44 "It is sown a natural body; it is raised a spiritual body. There is
a natural body, and there is a spiritual body."

It is as if Paul is piling verse upon verse to ensure that nobody can possibly miss the point—which, of course, traditional Christianity has missed completely.

45 "And so it is written, The first man Adam was made a living
soul; the last Adam was made a quickening spirit."

The first man was made a living soul; the second a quickening spirit. The job of the the second man was to give life to the first. But wasn't Adam *already* a glorious, immortal, perfect man? A *spiritual* man?

46 "Howbeit that was not first which is spiritual, but that which is
natural; and afterward that which is spiritual."

There it is in black and white. Adam wasn't spiritual!

47 "The first man is of the earth, earthy: the second man is the
Lord from heaven."

There are two men: Adam and Christ. It was God's intent in the original plan of creation that man's destiny be found in Christ, not in Adam. Just as Christ was the second Adam, so Adam was the first Christ. With one difference: he wasn't Christ! He was fleshly, subject to sin and corruption. He was the first draft, not the finished product. But no-one creates a first draft without a better version already embraced in their original plan.

48 "As is the earthy, such are they also that are earthy; and as is the heavenly, such are they also that are heavenly."

49 "As we have born the image of the earthy, we shall also bear the image of the heavenly."

50 "Now this I say, brethren, that flesh and blood cannot inherit the kingdom of God; neither doth corruption inherit incorruption."

Adam was not created one with Christ, as a new creation. The new creation is a joining of the first man and the second man. Adam was the first man; he could not possibly have been joined to the second. If he was, there would have been no need for the second. The second Adam's mission is to complete the first by *changing his nature* with his life and *developing his character* through trials into conformity with that of His own.

But, one might say, if this is true—if the whole matter is summed up in the simple phrase "I, if I were Christ . . . ," then how-come it is not more apparent? If the answer's really that simple, then why doesn't God just come right out and say it? I believe the answer lies in the fact that even as God has chosen to exercise us in the world, he has likewise chosen to exercise us by His word. How do you exercise someone? By opposing them, of course. I believe that one of God's goals in setting Himself against us in his word is to make us wrestle with Him. God's word resists us. It does not readily yield to us those things we most need. In fact it hides them. It hides them in Christ. It has hidden blessings in Christ that the Christian system have taught us are not even available. What are those things? Well, as sinners we need mercy, of course. And all would agree that the bible offers at least the possibility of mercy. But I would argue that we need much more than that. I would argue that we need from our heavenly Father the same things we need from our earthly fathers. Things like sympathy, empathy, compassion, understanding and affirmation. Moreover, we need two things from our heavenly Father that we cannot get from our earthly parents. They are justification and vindication. The bible does not easily concede any of these things, and nowhere is this fact more vividly reflected than in Calvinism.

## Justification

Calvinist theology will allow for no more than mercy. And this mercy is framed in terms that make clear why no more can be hoped for: You are an evil, odious creature, unworthy to even approach God. But in His unfathomable mercy, He placed all of your filthy, disgusting, vile sins on His Son, and punished them in Him, and now, through Him, and for His sake only, you may approach His throne of grace and receive mercy. If you are one of the elect. This is the grim picture in Calvinist theology.

But that's Calvinism. What about the bible? Does it offer anything beyond the possibility of mercy? I would argue that it does. But not on the surface. Dig a little deeper, however, and you will find that "he sympathizes with our weaknesses" and is "mindful of our frame, that we are but dust" (Heb. 4:15, Psalm 103:14). In fact, he does "not grieve willingly" (Lamentations 3:32–33).

Okay, so there's sympathy. But empathy? Understanding? Vindication? Surely I am asking too much now. Well, maybe and maybe not. These are all things we want; I would even suggest that they are things we need. And if so, then I would also suggest that no-one who God created for Himself will ever—or can ever—be denied them. Such a thing is not really possible in the very nature of things. Why would God make someone for Himself to whom he could never give the things he really needs? No, I believe those things can indeed be found. But not from a servile and unquestioning mindset. From this mindset, which accepts that Adam *should* have been able to outperform *Christ*, we can never expect more than mercy. But for those who dare to question that assumption, there is much more available. And it's not without reason that I use the word dare. You cannot "wrestle" these higher blessings out of God without showing some courage. In fact, you cannot do it without standing up to God. Servile and unquestioning, we can claim only mercy. But if we come to the bible insisting that it is reasonable, we can claim much more. We can claim the truth of "I, if I were Christ . . ." and all that it entails. Preston Eby writes:

> "Old Adam, the flesh, the carnal mind will never pass through the portals of Eden. The New Creation Man is he who enters and he enters with no dread of the Cherubim and the flaming sword upon him, for he is fully *justified*. There can be *no objection* to his entrance, for justification is being *declared righteous. . . .*"
> It may be shown by contrasting *condemnation* with *justification* that both acts are judicial and not executive. The act of granting "pardon" is an executive act, the act of a ruler—president, king, governor etc.—who grants reprieve to one pronounced "guilty" by a judge or jury simply because it pleases him to do so. He thereby restores to society one who is still *judicially guilty*, yet free to resume his place in society as a normal citizen. "Justification," on the

other hand, is the act of a judge, a forensic act, in which a judge pronounces the person arraigned as *free from guilt* and entitled to be treated as righteous according to the law. If "to condemn" does not mean "to make evil" then "to justify" does not mean "to make good." Therefore, since condemnation is judicial, so, also, justification. When the Bible says, "God *justifies* the believer," we are not at liberty to say that it means that He either pardons, forgives, or sanctifies him. It means, and can only mean that He pronounces him *just*—without fault . . .

Ah—to be justified means to be *acquitted*. Acquitted means to be declared by a court of law *not guilty—exonerated*! Justification means that you really *didn't do it*! Thus, justification relates not to forgiveness or pardon for the errors and sins of the *old nature*, but to the *standing and state of being of the new creation*. The New Man, born from above, *really didn't do it*! . . . "Whosoever is born of God doth not commit sin; for His seed remaineth in him: he cannot sin, because he is born of God" (I Jn. 3:9) . . .

Yes, old Adam was pronounced *guilty* and banished from Eden's fair Garden. But new Adam is declared *righteous* and may, therefore, stride boldly back into Paradise! We are now *justified* to *return to paradise . . .*"[3]

And this goes to the very crux of the matter. If a man is inherently evil, and his existence nothing more than a blight, then the best he can hope for is mercy. For all of those other things—compassion, understanding, sympathy, empathy—can only apply where there are mitigating circumstances. You can have no understanding for *pure* evil. You cannot sympathize with *pure* evil. And you certainly cannot empathize with someone who does something you would never do *even if you were that person*. It is this very perception of man—as—disease that governs Calvinist theology. The Calvinist insists that man is inherently evil. The evil we do, they point out, is all from us; the good is all from God. We may do good things, but the *real* us is bad. No. Justification insists on just the opposite. Justification insists it wasn't the *real* you doing the *bad*. We were created in God's image; Christ is the *real* us. After all, what does it mean to be created in Christ's image? The truth is that we cannot simply be *created* in God's image; we must be *conformed* into His image. Ask most preachers what it means to be created in Christ's image and they will say something like this: *Well, we are have been made like God in many ways. We can think, we can reason, we can love.* But that's not what it means to be created in Christ's image. Being able to love

3. Eby, "Echoes From Eden."

does not mean we are in His image; being unable to *not love* means we are in His image. Sinlessness is a character trait of the divine nature. Of course we were created with a certain capacity for love. A *dog* has a certain capacity for love. But were we created with the ability to love God the way Christ loves God? Of course not. This has to be developed. We must be conformed into the character of Christ. A man without Christ's character is no more in God's image than a wax figure of a man is in man's image. Likeness does not equal ability. The first is there from the start; the second must be developed. Adam had God's *likeness*; He did not have Christ's *ability*.

Traditional teaching has failed to understand that man is a vessel; he is defined by that which fills him. In and of itself a vessel is nothing. But the vessel is not to be condemned on this account. That's what it is; that's how God created it. To the extent that God fills man, then man cannot sin; to the extent that He doesn't fill him, he *must*. What conservative evangelical Christian is prepared to deny either half of that statement? Not one of them. And yet they deny it every time they insist that Adam could have resisted sin simply by virtue of his *own* glorious nature.

My former pastor once said we will spend eternity in heaven thanking God for not sending us to hell. But think of what an indictment of our existence this is! Even in heaven, we are not really where we *ought* to be. God made us to be with him forever where we *ought not to be*. We will spend eternity thanking Him for not hating us *as He ought to hate us*. Consider how badly this violates the foundation of Calvinist theology, namely, that God acts primarily to maximally display His glory. But doesn't God, in order to maximally display His glory, have to give the elect the very best that He could give them? And wouldn't that have to include the things that all creatures by nature want? Like respect and vindication? But how can He ever give those things to creatures that He has created with an inherently negative value? Does anyone prefer undeserved love to deserved love? If God could have created and developed the elect so as to *deserve* a place in heaven, and didn't, then how has He done His best for them?

Apparently, the Calvinist thinks the *best* God could do for them is to allow them a place in heaven, where they ought not to be, in order that they may spend eternity thanking God for allowing them in anyway. What a petty, childish tyrant they make out of God! He has everything, and yet His creatures, who He forces into existence, must regard every provision necessary to that existence, as an unfathomable, undeserved, supererogatory act of kindness, for which they are hopelessly in debt. He gives us lungs, but we don't deserve air; eyes, but we don't deserve sight; appetites; but we don't deserve food. But then how are they even gifts? Would we have ever *wanted* these things under those terms? They make God into the worse miser the mind can imagine. Whatever He gives He regards, in effect, as stolen. This is exactly how we would expect a two year old—and a deranged one at that—to behave should He be granted the power to do so. But what can the Calvinists do about it? If eternal torment is true, then this is what God is like. You can either accept it and worship Him for what He is, or you can go to hell. And part of accepting this version of God is accepting the fact that you have an inherently negative value. You deserve nothing. The slightest blessing is supererogatory. As a creature who is not God, and solely by virtue of that fact, you deserve only misery and contempt. And just to the extent He allows you anything better, to that extent you are a debtor.

This obsequious posture reflects a complete lack of understanding of the true meaning of justification. What is this justification—this *right* to enter paradise by virtue of Christ's righteousness—if not a *reversal* of the condemnation incurred by Adam's unrighteousness? What is it except a judicial decree from *God himself* of this fact: You, if you were me, should be as I am! Why were you condemned? Because you, if you were Adam, would have been just like him. Why are you justified? Because you, if you were Christ, would be just like him. *All* blessings are available in Christ—not just mercy! What kind of God would create you in such a way that your existence could never—for all eternity—be vindicated? What kind of a God would create you to forever dwell where you *ought not to be*? A God who knows the beginning from the end, and who arranges all things toward that end, could never participate in such a travesty. He would create you and arrange all the circumstances in such a way so as to ensure that you would ultimately wind up exactly where you ought to be. He would fit you for the end for which He made you, not for something else. He would not fit you for hell, and then, by a supererogatory act of mercy, allow you into Heaven. He would make you so that you *deserved* heaven. The means would serve the end. He would "subject you to vanity" that you might "learn obedience by the things suffered," and then He would grant you full access into the heavenly mansions. And that is exactly what God did. He made us all so that we would deserve heaven by *filling up the afflictions that are lacking in Christ.*

In other words, the saved sinner receives mercy, compassion, understanding, affirmation, sympathy, empathy, justification, and *vindication*!

His existence is vindicated. He was bad in Adam, but that wasn't the *real* him. Now, in Christ, who is the *real* us (Col. 3:4), and into whose image we are conformed (Rom. 8:29), we are who we were meant to be. Our creation is completed. We are "very good." (Genesis 1:31).

Nothing screams at us more loudly in our every day lives than the fact that the real man is not evil. The alcoholic, the addict, the junkie, the beggar, the bum, the glutton, the sluggard, the peddler, the pusher, the pimp, the prostitute, the pervert, and every other soul mired in the squalor of sin and depravity screams in his soul: But this isn't the *real* me! This is the very groaning of creation. It is the groan of *I, if I were Christ* . . . To this groaning the orthodox church system replies: It doesn't matter what you would be; only what you are. You are a sinner. That is the real you. You are doing exactly what you want to do. The groan comes back: *But if I were better, I wouldn't want to. If I were Christ, I'd be just like Him.* To the creation groaning, subjected to vanity, screaming in their souls for release—a release meant, by the way, to come through the *sons of God*—the Church system says: No, you are mistaken. That's the real you. And it is the condition in which you will be retained for all eternity. In order that God may punish you for *being in it.*

A correct understanding of the relationship between Christ and Adam reveals what a great lie this is. But we cannot discern this fact by employing the Calvinist hermeneutic. We cannot "go to the Bible with no prejudices and no presuppositions whatsoever" and discover this. We must go insisting on this *self evident*, philosophically unassailable, scientifically provable truth: *If I were Christ, I would be just like Him.* Going to the bible with humility is all well and good, and no Christian would suggest we do otherwise. But there are some things we must insist on. *To find truth we must have the humility to yield up to God those things we can't know, the courage to insist on those things we can know, and the wisdom to know the difference.* It is this lack of courage and wisdom that causes Calvinism to cling to a theology that does nothing to vindicate man and "vindicates" God in the face of suffering only by proposing that he *likes* it.

## Self Evident Truth Two: We Are All Brothers

Eckhart Tolle writes:

> Enlightenment means rising above thought, not falling back to a level below thought, to the level of an animal or a plant. In the

enlightened state, you will still use your thinking mind when needed, but in a much more focused and effective way than before.[4]

And what will this enlightenment yield? What truth proceeds from this place that is *above* reason?

Enlightenment is a state of wholeness, of being "at one" and therefore at peace. At one with life in its manifested aspect, the world, as well as with your deepest self and life unmanifested—at one with Being.[5]

How misguided Tolle must be, for the Calvinist assures us that true enlightenment should yield precisely the *opposite* state, one where we realize we are *not* all one, that it is not *inherently* better to love than to hate, or to forgive than to hold a grudge, for when God finally reveals the *truth*, that is to say, when he lifts the veil of election, we will see that God's glory is equally served by both sets of attitudes and that one of them is really no better than the other.

And yet by every conceivable appearance, the closer one moves toward true enlightenment, to that state of mind that transcends mere reason, the further away he moves from this way of thinking. The true sage, the shaman, the wiseman, the mystic, or just the really *good* guy, is one who seems to recognize the deep-rooted, organic, utterly *unprovisional* oneness of all men, whereas the most self-righteous, the legalistic, the cold-hearted, seem to move in the direction of a provisional love, one that comes off more like hate and admits to no real duty or affection or commitment to the objects of that love, but only to a duty to the God that commands it as a temporary exercise. And although some Calvinists may indeed exhibit generous spirits, it seems that they do so only in direct proportion to the degree that they act against, not with, their own beliefs.

## The Atonement

Tolle talks of At-one-ness. Enlightenment consists of realizing our oneness with man, God, the universe, and ourselves. It is coming to realize that we are all inextricably linked at an organic level and that all separation is an illusion. This is the universal testimony of those who have attained enlightenment. Nobody who attains this state, whether the sage, the shaman, the

4. Tolle, *The Power of Now*, 23.
5. Ibid., 15.

mystic, or the wiseman, believes that it is something other than this truth of the oneness of all things.

*The upward progression of human consciousness is marked by an increasing awareness of the universal brotherhood of all men and their organic oneness with each other, the universe, and God. It is true of all men of all faiths in all times, even in men who subscribe to doctrines that deny it, as evidenced by the fact that their own enhanced consciousness is displayed only to the extent that they ignore the implications of those doctrines.*

But does this idea, clearly popular with new-agers and the like, actually find expression in the bible? Actually, it not only finds expression, but it is at the very root of the gospel itself. Thomas Thayer writes:

> "The word 'Atonement' is one of those theological terms, the true meaning of which has been sadly perverted . . . It is a curious fact that this word, which occupies so large a space in theological literature . . . is found only once in the New Testament. Rom. V. 11. And the use of it in this passage is so directly in conflict with the meaning commonly attached to it, that it is a marvel how it ever came to signify substitution, or the suffering of Christ in the sense of satisfaction to the divine Justice. The meaning of the original word is wide enough from this idea, and is properly expressed in every other passage where it occurs by the English word "reconciliation . . . Originally, it was written as two words, joined by a hyphen, and pronounced thus, *at-one*, and the noun *at-one-ment*, meaning a state of *oneness* or unity."[6]

Of course it is the very denial of this fundamental truth that leads to some of the bizarre contrivances entertained by the Christian religious system. In opposition to this idea of organic unity, they will insist, among other things, that man is not made up of the same stuff of God, but rather was created by God out of nothing, and that God is not the Universal Father. We have already explored the latter issue; let's now take a look at the former.

## Created Out of Nothing

The idea that we are made of nothing is almost as ridiculous as that other gem foisted upon us by the orthodox system, namely, that *sin* came up out of nothing. Shirley C. Guthrie describes it this way:

6. Thayer, Theology of Universalism 123–124.

"Neither the literal nor the symbolic interpretation of Satan explains the origin of evil. Even if we think literally of a rebellion of angels that took place before creation, we only push the problem back one step and leave unanswered all the objections we have raised to attributing evil to any creature of God. How could *any* of God's creatures rebel against their God when *all* that God creates is good?"[7]

That is Christian doctrine at its finest. Sin came from nothing. *We* came from nothing. But of course sin did not come from nothing; nor did we come from nothing. We came from God. There's no such thing as *nothing*. And if such a thing did exist, some hole in space devoid of every conceivable form of matter and energy, it still wouldn't prove that we could be created out of it, for something can't come out of nothing; this is the fact employed by the religious establishment to prove the existence of God in the first place! If God is everywhere, then where exactly can we find nothing? We would have to find somewhere that God Himself did not exist.

No, God did not create us out of nothing. He created us out of Himself! That *doesn't* mean we *are* God and He is us, but it does mean, at the very least, that the stuff we're made of came from God. It means there exists an *indivisible* link between the Creator and the creature. And to imagine that it could be otherwise, as conservative Christians have, is too ludicrous for words. *Of Course* the Creator and the creature are one in a far more profound way than human fathers, or *procreators,* and *their* offspring, and yet no-one, including conservative Christians, would deny *that* organic unity and the obligations it entails.

"... by him all things consist." (Col 1:17)

"For of him, and through him, and to him, are all things ..." (Romans 11:36)

"For in him we live, and move, and have our being; as certain of your own poets have said, For we are also his offspring." (Acts 17:28)

Everything we believe about who we are and where we're going goes back to what we believe about where and *what* we came from. Did we come from God? Or from nothing? Is He our Father? Or only our *Creator*? Are we, in a fundamental sense, one with Him and our neighbor? Or are we just so many disparate fragments of matter and energy who bear no organic

7. Guthrie, Christian Doctrine 182.

relationship to each other and our Creator? Is *At-one-ness* a new-age contrivance that bears no relationship to biblical Christianity? Or is it the very heart of the gospel, the very thing Christ procured for us at the cross? The bible answers thus:

> "Now all things are of God, who has reconciled us to Himself through Jesus Christ, and has given us the ministry of reconciliation, that is, that God was in Christ reconciling the world to Himself, not imputing their trespasses to them, and has committed to us the word of reconciliation." (II Corinthians 5:18,19)

## Self-Evident Truth Three: Man Is Not Inherently Good or Evil

In his classic book *Christian Doctrine*, Shirley C. Guthrie writes:

> "Neither the literal nor the symbolic interpretation of Satan explains the origin of evil. Even if we think literally of a rebellion of angels that took place before creation, we only push the problem back one step and leave unanswered all the objections we have raised to attributing evil to any creature of God. How could *any* of God's creatures rebel against their God when *all* that God creates is good?"[8]

How indeed? How can we rebel when God made us good? The answer is *self-evident*. We can't. It is this need to pin the responsibility for evil on the creature rather than the Creator that has prevented Christians from understanding the nature of both man and of evil. Regarding the origin of evil, Preston Eby writes:

> "The answer is so simple, so plain, so basic, we blush and bow our heads with shame even for the asking! How can you create darkness? Just by turning off the light! Anyone can perform this simple feat at any hour of the day or night. The sequence is totally correct, as we read in Isa. 45:7, "*I form the light*, and *create darkness*." The initial state is light. God is light and He was before all things—eternal, omnipresent Light. Withdraw that light and there is darkness. But the light came first, and therefore is always able to swallow up the darkness into light itself again. "The light still shines in the darkness and the darkness has never put it out" (Jn. 1:5, Phillips). The light will always conquer darkness, but darkness

8. Ibid., 181.

shall never conquer light. But to create darkness—it is only necessary to *withdraw* the light!"[9]

Darkness occurs in exact proportion to the absence of light. It cannot be otherwise. Moreover, man himself cannot shut off or dim the light. That's because it is only darkness that would make him want to do so in the first place. "Whomsoever is born of God . . . cannot sin." (1 John 3:9)

There's a big difference between being created in God's image and being born of God. Christ was born of God. Adam was not. Indeed this point is emphasized so strongly in 1 Cor. 15 that it's a wonder anyone missed it. The entire passage insists that Adam was created with a lack. Light was withheld. The result was darkness. Corruption (1 Cor. 15:42). Weakness (1 Cor. 15:43). Dishonour (1 Cor. 15:43). This occurred in exact proportion to the amount of light that God withheld. Not one bit less. Not one bit more. But of course the entire doctrine of original sin is based on the idea that there was indeed a *disproportion* between the amount of light withheld and the amount of darkness that ensued. The theory goes that however God made Adam—perfect or close to it—He made him better than he turned out. This, of course, is pure nonsense. It does what all worldly thought systems do—it makes a God of man and a man of God. It pits Creator against creature and has the creature prevail. It imagines that cause and effect in the spiritual realm will not follow as tightly as it does in every other. Again, this is nonsense. For the spiritual realm, as surely as the physical, operates according to the same precise laws that govern the rest of the universe. They are no less fixed, no less controlled, in every way, by God. There is a law of sin and death (Rom. 8:2) that governs the conduct of the unregenerate:

"*They that are in the flesh cannot please God.*" (Romans 8:8)

And a law of life that governs the conduct of the regenerate:

"*Whomsoever is born of God . . . cannot sin*" (1 John 3:9)

We can no more disobey these laws than a falling safe can disobey the laws of gravity. It falls exactly as quickly as the law of gravity dictates. Not one second slower. Not one second faster. There's no gap between cause and effect. It all proceeds in precise accordance with God's laws. It cannot be otherwise. The bible says as much when it declares "O LORD, I know the way of man is not in himself; it is not in man who walks to direct his own steps" (Jeremiah 10:23). How does a man direct his steps? By the light in

9. Eby, "The Restitution of All Things."

his path, of course. "Thy word is a lamp unto my feet, and a light unto my path." (Psalm 119:105) But who controls the light? The bible answers "For with thee is the fountain of life: in thy light we see light" (Psalm 36:9). In *His* light we see light. If our light is dim it can mean only one thing: He dimmed *His* light. We do not control the light. We can't turn it on and we can't turn it off. It is not *in* a man to direct his steps.

The Calvinist is ignorant not of the form of these facts, but of their substance. They will concede that man's will is not free, but insist that, free or not, he is still guilty because he is still *evil*. But this is a cop-out. Moreover, it involves a complete misapprehension of the the nature of man, or, worse yet, it *blames* man for his nature. The Calvinists are correct; man *is* evil. Man *is* selfish. But they ignore the fact that this is a flaw that is inherent in the very nature of a created being. They do not understand what it means to be a creature. The fact is that all things in the universe are motivated by one thing: Self Interest. And this includes God Himself. The difference between Adam and Christ was not that Adam cared only for himself and Christ only for others. Hogwash! The difference is that Adam *didn't know what was in his own best interests*. But make no mistake; in both cases—that of Christ and that of man—self interest is the governing factor, the factor that inclines the will one way or the other. The bible makes no bones about the fact that it is always God's own good *pleasure* that serves as the impetus for all of His creative and even redemptive activities. Unlike man, however, His pleasure is unselfish. Why? Because through the force of His will he opts for the good rather than the evil? Of course not. God is unselfish because he already *has* all that He could ever want. Man doesn't. We are told to give out the overflow of our hearts. That is the very essence of Christian agape love. God, as the Source of all good things, has a built-in overflow. He needs nothing. He can be given nothing. He can only derive joy from giving. This is not so with man; indeed man, by his very nature, mostly derives joy by *receiving*. To blame man for this is to demonstrate the worst kind of ignorance about the very nature not only of man and evil, but of God Himself.

## Self-Evident Truth Four: God Subjected Us; God Will Free Us

The Miriam-Webster dictionary defines theodicy as: defense of God's goodness and omnipotence in view of the existence of evil. Note the phrase: the *existence* of evil. Not its endless perpetuity. Not the idea that it will be forever preserved in a corner of the universe called hell. Not the notion that it will increase continuously for as long as God shall live. No, its mere *existence* is a puzzle in and of itself. Theodicy is the proper pursuit of philosophers, moralists, artists, etc . . . , most of whom operate from the premise that evil, while enduring historically through successive generations, does indeed end for each individual at the point of death.

The theologian, however, has no such luxury; hence the difficulty of his task is compounded exponentially. His task is twofold: defense of God's goodness and omnipotence in view of the existence of evil in *this* life . . . to be followed by eternal misery in the *next*. Of course one can choose to justify the latter by appealing to the former. We are punished in the next life for the evil we do in this one. But how do you defend the fact that evil exists at all? Here is where the theologian encounters a problem. Why? Because the *self-evident* defense for the existence of evil in this life—namely, that it is *temporary*—is not available to them due to the fact that traditional Christianity teaches that it will go on forever; hence the most obvious, most convincing, and indeed the *only* justification for the existence of evil cannot be employed. Consequently, we have ended up with two theological systems that cannot offer us an adequate theodicy.

Arminianism tells us that *man*, not God, is the author of suffering; hence there cannot really be a good reason for it. It can only be regarded as an unintended result that God incorporated into his plan. It was not part of the *original* plan. It is not something *He* planned. It is not, therefore, a means to an end; after all, the *same* end was meant to be achieved without it. At least this is how the Arminians see it. Their theology can be summed up this way: "God, who *could* have done it (created evil), *wouldn't* have done it; therefore man, who *couldn't* have done it, *must* have done it." Or, to put it another way—*mystery*.

Calvinism, on the other hand, takes a different approach. Calvinists do believe God intended evil to exist. But the reason they propose is hardly one that offers hope or purpose in the face of evil. They believe God desired that evil exist in order to punish it. For the vast majority of men it serves no purpose whatsoever. Their theology can be summed up this way: "God, who *needed* evil, nonetheless bears no responsibility for its existence; nor did he create man in a way that guaranteed that He (God) would get what he needed; it just sort of happened by a happy coincidence." Or, to put it another way—*mystery*. Fortunately, there is a third option.

> "For the creature was made subject to vanity, not willingly, but
> by reason of Him who hath subjected the same, in hope, Because
> the creature itself also shall be delivered from the bondage to cor-
> ruption into the glorious liberty of the children of God" (Romans
> 8:20–21)

An adequate theodicy is not possible so long as we ascribe to God evil motives or to man the power to frustrate God's intentions. Either evil came from God or it has no point. Either he intends to destroy it or it has no justification. No reasonable person can argue with this. There is one way and one way only to vindicate God's justice in the face of evil, and that is to insist on the scriptural position that God created evil for a limited time and for wise purposes. It is the only reason that that resonates with our deepest longings, and our sense of reason and conscience. It is the only reason that is fixed, divinely ordained, not based on contingency, applicable to all men, and destined to result in the progression of all souls from death to life, from vanity to glory, from the transient to the immutable. Anything less is not worthy of a God that deserves to be worshiped.

I have mentioned this verse many times. Sadly, this verse, which is central to Universalism, is all but ignored outside of it. In fact, the popular theology does not even believe this verse applies to man. Sadly, this bias has crept into the way the verse has been translated. This is the way my King James bible renders the verse:

> "For the creature was made subject to vanity, not willingly, but
> by reason of him who hath subjected the same, in hope, Because
> the creature itself also shall be delivered from the bondage of cor-
> ruption into the glorious liberty of the children of God." (Romans
> 8:20–21)

There are two problems with this translation. First, the letter *h* in the word him is not capitalized. It should be. The word is Him, not him. Sec-ondly, the word translated creature in verse twenty is the same word that was translated creation in verse twenty one. These errors in translation have contributed to an interpretation of the verse that goes something like this:

> "For the animals were made subject to vanity, not willingly, but by
> reason of man who hath subjected the same, in hope, Because the
> animals themselves also shall be delivered . . ."

But the verse *is* talking about all of creation and I will attempt to prove it by taking a closer look at two of the phrases in this important passage.

## For the Creature

The assertion has been made that the phrase *for the creature* concerns animals, not man. This interpretation is without any foundation. It may indeed include them, but there's no reason to believe it is *limited* to them. 1 Col. 1:15 says "Who is the image of the invisible God, the firstborn of every creature . . ." There are two things to note:

1. The word creature is used with reference to man and

2. Christ, while the firstborn of all creation in general, is more specifically, the firstborn of mankind.

It's hard to see how one can argue that man is not in view here. Moreover, verse 23 states that "the gospel . . . was preached to every *creature* which is under heaven . . ." To whom is the gospel preached—man or animals?

The book of Ecclesiastes deals a great deal with man's subjection to vanity. In fact, it is in the very context of a discussion of man's vanity that Solomon compares us to beasts, saying: "I said in my heart concerning the estate of the sons of men, that God might manifest them, and that *they might see that they themselves are but beasts* . . . so that a man hath no pre-eminence above a beast: for all is vanity" (Eccl. 3:18). Here Solomon points to the fact that man and animals share the same fate as the very cause of *our* vanity, not that of the *animal's*. Yet the traditional view would have us believe that it is the animals groaning because *we* have dragged them down into death *with us*.

Moreover, when one considers that vanity entails the idea of transitiveness, it becomes all but impossible to imagine that the bible had animals primarily in view when talking about creatures being made subject to vanity. One need only consider the respective natures of man and animals to understand this. Man has a desire for permanence and transcendence; animals do not. For an animal to be subjected to vanity is a minor inconvenience; for man it is a calamity that places his body at war with his spirit, his reality at odds with his deepest desires. Karen Armstrong writes: "We are meaning-seeking creatures. Dogs, as far as we know, do not agonize about the canine condition, worry about the plight of dogs in other parts of the world, or try to see their lives from a different perspective."[10]

The bible says God subjected us to vanity in *hope*. Hope implies a reason. Apparently the state of vanity—impermanence—will yield some kind of fruit. It will teach us lessons and accomplish things that God deemed

10. Armstrong, *A Short History of Myth*, 2.

necessary before we can be released from this condition. Man is *exercised* by it (Eccl. 3:10). Are animals? Are they learning lessons from their condition? Are they growing, maturing, evolving in any way? Is their experience with mortality teaching them anything about immortality? Of course not. Animals are blissfully unaware of their mortal conditions from the time they are born to the time they die. For man, however, death is a constant backdrop. It colors his every thought, word, and deed. Truly man has been made subject to vanity. Truly he needs to be released from it.

## Made Subject to Vanity, Not Willingly

Was man subjected to vanity? We will let the bible answer.

> "So I am made to possess months of vanity . . ." (Job 17:3)

> " . . . my days are vanity. What is man . . . that thou shouldest . . . try him every moment?" (Job 7:16–18)

> "Why is light given to a man whose way is hid, and whom God hath hedged in?" (Job 4:23)

> "I have seen the travail, which God hath given to the sons of men to be exercised in it." (Eccl. 3:10)

Notice how these verses contradict the idea that man—through his supposed free will—subjected himself and the animals to vanity. Yes, man's immediate sin brings immediate consequences. But God did not arrange His long-term plan base on man's short-term, short-sighted, selfish decisions. Sin plays a part in our subjection to vanity, but God plays a *bigger* part. Robert Morey writes:

> Where should we begin when studying God's sovereignty and man's responsibility? Should we begin with man and establish his free will and then define divine sovereignty in such a way it does not conflict with man? Or should we begin with God and His free will and then develop our understanding of man from that viewpoint? We must begin where Scripture begins . . . The Bible begins with GOD. He is the great I AM, the Alpha . . . Omega, the Beginning . . . End.[11]

Tradition has interpreted Romans 8:20 by giving man's will the preeminence. It has put man's will on a par with God's, making him co-equal

---

11. Beauchemin, *Hope Beyond Hell*, 38.

with God. Yes, man was the proximate cause of sin entering, and death through sin. But God was the *root* cause. And as any psychologist will tell you, it's the root cause that matters. Until you get to that, you are just tinkering around the margins. Nothing gets resolved until the root cause is exposed. Then we know the cause of—and the solution to—the whole problem. That's what God gives us with Romans 8:20. Unfortunately, man will not accept it. He will not admit that God caused the problem. It must have been him. It had to be something he did. Again, we go back to Job. Just as when God removed Satan from the picture in the book of Job—revealing Himself as the cause of Job's suffering—so He removes man from the picture in Romans 8:20—once again revealing Himself as the cause of man's suffering. But man keeps putting himself back in. Just as he keeps putting Satan back into the book of Job (as the cause of the problem). Just as he keeps insisting on a doctrine of original sin in Romans 5:12 as opposed to a doctrine of *imputed* sin. Every time God tries to insert Himself as the cause, man tries to argue. This is nothing more than silliness and false piety. As if God needed us to defend Him!

Another verse that clearly tells us that it was God who subjected man to vanity is 1 Cor. 15:42: "It is sown in corruption." Compare this with the language of Romans 8:21: "For the creature was made subject to vanity, not willingly . . ." The obvious question here is: Who sowed us? The obvious answer is: God.

The idea that the groaning of the creation in view is that of the animals is easily dispelled by a simple glance at verse 23 , where the groaning clearly applies to man. If saved man is groaning, and the animals are groaning, then exactly how is it that the *unsaved* masses of the world are *not* groaning? They must be excluded from this groaning creation for one reason and one reason only—if they are allowed in, then it means that they too will one day be saved. And we all know *that* can't be true. And so men have used every ploy in the book to keep them out. But the bible will not allow it. Notice verse 21: "For we have known that all the creation doth groan together, and doth travail in pain together till now." Does this seem to be excluding anyone, much less the vast majority of mankind? Who groans the loudest—animals or men? Who *travails in pain*? "I have seen the travail, which God hath given to the sons of men to be exercised in it." (Eccl. 3:10) "For he doth not afflict willingly nor grieve the children of men." (Lamentations 3:33) The sons of *men*. That means all men. And all creation. For as the wise man said "I said in my heart concerning the estate of the sons of men, that

## Part 3: **God's Mercy Will Extend to All**

God might manifest them, and that *they might see that they themselves are but beasts* . . . (Eccl. 3:18).

# 10

# The Judgment Verses

IT IS WITH GREAT reluctance that I embark upon this particular part of the book, namely, the part that deals specifically with certain verses and proposes a certain way to interpret them. The reason for this reluctance should be obvious to the reader by this point. I did not set out to write a book arguing the case for Universalism, per se. By that I mean I did not set out to make the case for this or that interpretation of this or that verse or verses. Instead I have set out to redefine the proper role of biblical exegesis. I have tried to prove that this endeavor, as it is currently understood, namely, as a way of discerning God's attitude toward us by studying and comparing various verses, is doomed to failure. It is doomed to failure because our interpretation of scripture will depend on our antecedent understanding of God's attitude toward us. For instance, how do we interpret the lake of fire?

Calvinism reasons thusly:

1. God sends men into the lake of fire

2. The lake of fire is eternal torment

3. Therefore, God is an eternal tormentor

4. Therefore, God is not the father of all men

But the problem is that there are many different ways of interpreting the lake of fire and those interpretations depend on *how we understand God as Father.* In other words, the Calvinist says: Number four is true because number one, two, and three is true. But the truth is that number four is true *only if we interpret numbers one through three in light of number four.* Interpret numbers one through three in light of the idea that God is everyone's father and you come up with a totally different understanding of the lake of fire.

We must first decide if God is the Universal Father. And we can't do this by reasoning from the verses touching on other subjects, like, for instance, the lake of fire. No, the only way to make this determination is to see what the bible itself says about the *very issue of God as Father*. For this *does not depend on interpretation*. Not if the verses plainly say He is our father or plainly say He's not.

Which brings me to the reason for this chapter. Perhaps one might be willing to concede that from a purely rational standpoint my arguments have some merit. Of course, they might say, our vision of God will color our interpretation of scripture. Moreover, they might even concede that one could, if one were so inclined, interpret God as the Universal Father. It is at that point, however, that they may draw the line. God is love, fine. God is our father, fine. But the verses—even though open to various interpretations which *may depend on our antecedent visions of God—nevertheless* simply do not allow for Universal Salvation. They are simply too decisive to allow for such an interpretation. It is to address that objection that I found it necessary to include this chapter. It is not an exhaustive study of every verse pertaining to judgment. I am simply trying to show that my interpretation of the bible is not prohibited by the judgment verses.

## Christ's Punishment: Hell or Death?

Is the wages of sin death? Or is it hell? Put aside for a moment the Universalist position that death is the pathway to life and that all will eventually be saved through it and what you have here is basically a debate between the Traditionalist and the Annihilationist. How can we establish which view is correct? I would like to suggest from the outset that such a thing is impossible. That is because in trying to decide between the two, we will encounter the same problem as we encounter in trying to decide between Universalism and Traditionalism. That problem, of course, is that each camp will read the verses in light of their antecedent opinions about the character of God. Only in this debate there is no real tiebreaker. The Annihilationist cannot appeal to a fundamentally different conception of God to support his position. The truth is that both his God and the traditionalist God create the unsaved in order to destroy them; the difference comes down to a disagreement on the nature of that destruction. It is a difference in degree, not in *kind*; hence there is nothing in the bible to substantiate it or to refute it. It all comes down to how a person interprets a particular verse based on his opinion about the *extent of God's bloodlust*. There is nothing else separating the two camps. In view of this, I am making the following disclaimer: *I realize that every verse offered in the ensuing argument that argues for death as opposed to eternal torment can also be understood as depicting eternal torment rather than death. The interpretation will depend entirely on one's antecedent understanding of the character of God.*

Nevertheless. The Universalist *does* insist that the wages of sin is death; hence if he cannot demonstrate that this is at least *consistent* with the biblical witness, he cannot defend his position. That is what I will now attempt to do.

If the wages of sin is hell rather than death, we should expect to find the most vivid demonstration of this fact in the punishment of the person who came to pay that wage. Do we? Not at all. It is at this most pivotal of all places that we find the least evidence for hell. Here—where "hell" is encountered head-on—is precisely where all of the language of hell falls as silent as the grave itself. And that silence is pierced by a thunderous cacophony consisting solely of the language of death. Edward Fudge observed:

> "The bible exhausts the vocabulary of dying in speaking of what happened to Jesus. He "*died* for our sins" (1 Cor. 15:3). He laid down his "*life*" (John 10:15). He was *destroyed* (Matthew 27:20) or *killed* (Acts 3:15). Jesus compared his own death to the *dissolution* of a kernel of wheat in the same passage that mentions losing one's *life* rather than loving it to find life eternal (1 John 12:23–26). Jesus "*poured out His life* unto death . . ." By every indication if Christ didn't rise from the dead, it would have been the end of him and of those who died in him. 1 Corinthians 15:13 states: "But if there be no resurrection of the dead, then Christ is not risen. Then they which are fallen asleep in Christ are perished."[1]

Upon what basis do Traditionalists insist that Christ suffered eternal torment in hell? By starting with an antecedent belief that *hell* is the penalty for sin and then reading it back into every one of the above-mentioned verses of scripture that *do not mention hell* and *surely would if such a thing were true.*

It's a fact that Old Testament sacrifices were not tormented; they were killed. And by every indication this was the fate Christ suffered on the

---

1. Fudge, *The Fire That Consumes*, 230.

cross. He became a curse for us (Galatians 13:13), and shed his blood for us (Hebrews 9:14). In Christ—the revelation of God's wrath—we find the language of death (Romans 6:23), resurrection (1 Cor. 15:42), reconciliation (Romans 5:10), washing, sanctification, and justification (1 Cor. 6:11), intercession (Heb. 9:15), blood (1 Cor. 11:25), redemption (Heb. 9:12), purification (Heb. 9:23), and union with God (1 Thess. 4:17), but nothing whatsoever of weeping and gnashing of teeth, fire and brimstone, or worms and maggots. In God's clearest, dearest, most intimate revelation of Himself and His wrath, we find only the language of the two polar opposites that God set before us from the beginning—life and death. The pronouncement in Romans 6:23—"The wages of sin is death"—seems to be God's final word on the subject of His wrath as revealed in Jesus Christ.

If indeed we can find no evidence that Christ suffered either eternal torment and we *know* He did not suffer annihilation, then we must admit one very clear and incontestable fact: Christ died and was *resurrected*. From this follows another very clear and incontestable fact: if God requires anyone to experience either eternal torment or annihilation, then He requires a punishment greater than that which Christ endured, which is to say, a punishment greater than His law allows. Hence the Universalist—so often accused of being unbiblical—is actually building his theology on a much firmer foundation than the Traditionalist or the Annihilationist, a foundation that takes into account what actually happened at the cross rather than one that deals in unreasonable speculation.

The problem is one of trying to make the cross conform to an antecedent opinion. The eternal tormentor believes the penalty for sin is eternal torment, so they must look for eternal torment at the cross, even though it cannot be found. The annihilationist believes the penalty for sin is eternal death, and so they must look for eternal death at the cross, even though it cannot be found. The Universalist—who is so "unbiblical"—believes the penalty for sin is death. Period. Followed by eternal life. He does not have to look for this at the cross; it is impossible to miss.

## Hell

Does the bible teach hell? Most definitely. The question is: What is it? Is it even a valid question, or is the answer self-evident? Can we establish grounds for questioning the traditional understanding of hell? And if we can, are those grounds clear and obvious, or strained and esoteric? In other words, is there a Prima-facie case for at least doubting the traditional understanding of hell as a place of eternal, conscious torment? I believe there is.

Hell is mentioned twelve times in the bible. Except for a passing reference in James, it always occurs in the gospels, and is always directed at Jews. It is never used in the epistles or the book of Acts. In those books we find judgment described in terms of death or destruction. Never hell. Not once. Why the discrepancy? Why do the gospels speak of hell, but the rest of the New Testament only of death or destruction? Why is this word, employed often in the gospels, *never* employed outside of them? There may be more than one answer to this question. I will, however, pose one possibility: Either death and destruction means hell or hell means death and destruction. Which is it? To answer the question, we must ask two other questions:

1. Did Gehenna, in it's normal usage, include death and destruction?

2. Did death, in its normal usage, include eternal torment?

Perhaps I phrased the first question unfairly. Of course Gehenna *included* death and destruction. The real question is: was it *limited* to death and destruction, or did it carry additional connotations? The fact is that it *did* carry additional connotations. The question then becomes: Were those additional connotations so extensive and so inherent in the term as to require that Gehenna, in it's normal usage, could not be compatible with death in it's normal usage? And if Gehenna *could* mean either death and destruction *or* eternal torment, which meaning did Christ have in mind when he employed the term?

Before proceeding, one might question if this is even a fair approach. Why not start from the other end? Why not try to establish whether or not death could mean eternal torment? Especially when it's used in ways that at least *imply* something beyond mere physical death. This is a valid point. Death in the New Testament often does imply something beyond mere death. How to resolve this issue? I will suggest that there is a middle ground—that death and Gehenna—both mean approximately the same thing—a disgraceful death. To die unsaved.

You will notice that I am using the word Gehenna rather than hell. This is not by accident.

All experts agree that hell is a translation of the word Gehenna. Not all agree on the relevance of this fact. I believe it is relevant. Whereas hell can only mean one thing, Gehenna can mean as many as five.

1. Gehenna can be understood as death by fire.

2. Gehenna can be understood as a synonym for calamity—either national or personal—that is terrible, to be sure, but falls short of eternal torment.

3. Gehenna can be understood as finite punishment in the afterlife

4. Gehenna can be understood as annihilation

5. Gehenna can be understood as eternal, conscious torment

Canon Farrar's exhaustive study of the issue led him to conclude:

> "For Gehenna was a technical term. It was a Hebrew term and not a Greek term. And yet exactly because it was technical and because no Greek term could serve as its equivalent, our Lord and the Apostles would not translate it into Greek, but they presented it, as it was, in its precise technical meaning, and only transliterated it from Hebrew into Greek letters;—as though He and they meant, in the most express manner, to prevent it from being mingled up with misleading conceptions which were alien from it . . . By neglecting that example we use a word which always means endless . . . punishment, as our substitute for a word which, to a Jew, nearly always meant an intermediate, a remedial, a metaphorical punishment, and above all, a punishment which was normally regarded as terminable."[2]

If in fact Farrar's claim is even close to true, then we must admit that hell did not *have* to mean endless punishment. It could mean something closer to what the authors of the epistles *seemed* to have in mind. The question is: Which *version* of Gehenna did Christ teach? Noted theologian Thomas Thayer wrote:

> "The first time Christ uses the word *Gehenna* is in Matt. v 22, 29, 30. But not a word of preparation or notice that now, for the first time, the terrible dogma is announced on divine authority. He speaks as calmly as if He were wholly unconscious of the burden of such a revelation; and the people seem equally unmoved under the awful declaration. And what is singular, it is not presented by itself, in a positive form, unmixed with anything else, as its importance most surely demanded; but is slipped in merely as a comparative illustration, among other judgments, of the greater moral demands of the Gospel, and the strictness with which it enforced obedience. They, the Jews, had said, "Whosoever shall kill, shall be in danger of the judgment;" but Christ says, whosoever is

2. Farar, *Mercy and Judgment*, ch 8.

angry with his brother without cause, is in danger of a punishment equal to that of the judgment (the inferior court of seven judges); and whosoever shall say to his brother, Raca (a term of contempt, shallow-brain or blockhead), shall be in danger of a punishment equal to that inflicted by the council (the superior court of seventy judges, which took cognizance of capital crimes); but whosoever shall say, "Thou fool, shall be in danger of hell-fire," or of a punishment equal in severity to the fire of Gehenna. Now, if Christ used the term *Gehenna* to reveal endless woe, and that for the first time, would He not have said this, and fixed forever the meaning of the word? And yet not the slightest intimation do we have of any such new and awful meaning. The Jews were familiar with it, and used it constantly to symbolize any great punishment or judgment coming on the earth; and they must of course suppose He used it as they did, since He gave them no notice to the contrary. If, therefore, He did give it the new signification of endless punishment after death, they could not understand Him, and He failed of His purpose for want of such explanation as they, and we, had a right to expect. But there is another consideration deserving notice. The difference between the sinfulness of saying Raca or Blockhead, and Fool, is hardly great enough to warrant such a difference in punishment as is involved in the supposition. Townsend justly says, to imagine that Christ, for such a slight distinction as Raca and Thou fool, would instantly pass from such a sentence as the Jewish Sanhedrin would pronounce, to the awful doom of eternal punishment in hell-fire, is what cannot be reconciled to any rational rule of faith, or known measure of justice."[3]

It should also be noted that of the twelve times Gehenna is used it is never accompanied by a mention of torment. Christ never once employed the phrase "weeping and gnashing of teeth" with regard to Gehenna. This, combined with the fact that the word is never addressed to the Gentiles in the epistles or in the Acts of the Apostles, constitutes a strong case for taking the word to mean something less than eternal torment.

In closing, there are twelve reasons to doubt the traditional doctrine of hell. They are as follows:

1. Christ never used the term to Gentiles

2. The Acts and the epistles only refer to hell once—a passing reference in James.

3. The bible says the wages of sin is death

3. Thayer, *The Origin and History of the Doctrine of Endless Punishment*, ch 5.

4. Christ did not suffer eternal torment

5. Christ never said he came to save anyone from hell

6. Life and death are contrasted dozens of times; never life and eternal torment

7. The Old Testament never mentions eternal torment

8. Old Testament sacrifices were killed, not tormented

9. Of the twelve times hell is mentioned, it is never used in connection with the word torment or words indicating torment

10. Hell goes against the character of God as revealed in Christ

11. Hell would nullify the promises of the bible to save all men

12. The gospel means good news. If Christ represented a judgment infinitely greater than that threatened in the Old Testament, than His ministry would not have been good news; it would have been bad news.

## The Lake of Fire

We will not dwell on the topic of hell. Christians believe one of two things:

1. Hell is the lake of fire, or

2. Hell is to be swallowed up by the lake of fire.

In either case the lake of fire is more important; if it can be established that the lake of fire is not a place of eternal torment, then hell is not eternal torment. So what about the lake of fire? Doesn't the bible clearly teach that it's forever? Rev. 21:10: "And the devil that deceived them was cast into the lake of fire and brimstone, where the beast and the false prophet are, and shall be tormented day and night forever and ever."

People infer from that verse that man, like Satan, will be tormented forever in the lake of fire. It seems to me, however, that one could just as easily infer the opposite from the fact that Rev. 20:15, which shows man cast into the lake of fire, says nothing about torment. After all, was the bible written for man or devils? Whose fate is primarily at issue? Who is reading these words for clues about their eternal destiny? Man or the devils? Isn't it strange that God would tell us exactly what happens to Satan in the lake of fire, but remain silent about man? Why would God be more explicit about Satan's fate in the fire than our own? If both man *and* Satan are to be tormented in the fire forever, wouldn't God either:

> Tell us that *man* is tormented, and leave us to infer Satan's fate, or
>
> Tell us that both man *and* Satan are tormented forever?

But instead we get this curious anomaly of God telling us that *Satan* is tormented forever and remaining silent about *us*. Is the reason perhaps that we do not share the same fate? Would this not be the most rationale explanation? Could it be that man's fate in the fire is found elsewhere in the bible?

The following five facts—and there are *many* more—argue strongly that the lake of fire is not designed to torment man forever.

1. Both 1 Cor. 2:13 and Rev. 20:11 state that "every man's work is to be judged by fire." The bible says every fact is to be established by two witnesses, or, to put it another way, to compare spiritual things with spiritual (1 Cor. 2:13). These two verses contain identical language. Note the specifics of each verse:

> Every man
>
> Every man's *works*
>
> Every man's works to be *judged*
>
> Every man's works to be judged by *fire*

A perfect spiritual match. And what does 1 Cor. 3:13–15 say about that fire? It says it will *save* every man. Moreover, the *exact* same language is employed in Zeph. 3:8–9, where God *devours the nations in fire* to *save* them. Another perfect spiritual match.

2. After the "nations" are cast into the lake of fire, we see them entering the New Jerusalem (Rev. 21:24, 26; 22:2). Tradition tells us these "nations" are the saints. The bible, however, never describes the nations as saints; the saints are always those *taken out* from the nations. Again, there's no spiritual match to support the traditional position.

3. Tradition offers no explanation for the open gates of the heavenly city. Compare the language of Revelations with Isaiah 60:10 and we see that the open gates represent an ongoing march of the nations into the New Jerusalem. Again, a perfect spiritual match.

4. Tradition tells us the lake of fire is everlasting punishment. But a comparison of Luke 12:46 and Rev. 21:8 indicates the opposite.

"The Lord of that servant will come in a day when he looketh not . . . and will appoint him his portion with the unbelievers . . ." (Luke 12:46)

"But the unbelieving . . . shall have their part in the lake [of fire]." (Rev. 21:8)

The servant of Luke 12 goes into the lake of fire. But for how long?

"And that servant, which knew his lord's will, and prepared not himself . . . shall be beaten with many stripes. But he that knew not . . . shall be beaten with few stripes."

Here we see that the punishment is limited. There are few stripes and there are many, according to the each man's faithfulness. Moreover, what does the bible say about stripes?

"Forty stripes he may give him, and not exceed: lest, if he should exceed, and beat him above these with many stripes, then thy brother should seem vile unto thee." (Deuteronomy 25:3)

Again, it's simply a matter of finding spiritual matches.

5. Just as limited stripes is inconsistent with eternal punishment, so is ongoing sin, such as lying, murdering, and hate-mongering. And yet that, according to Young's Literal Concordance, is exactly what will be going on in the lake of fire.

"Happy are those doing His commands that the authority shall be theirs unto the tree of life, and by the gates they may enter into the city; and without [are] the dogs, and the sorcerers, and the whoremongers, and the murderers, and the idolaters, and everyone who *is loving and is doing* a lie." (Rev. 22:13)

If we would only take God at His word, that He keeps His own law (Psalm 138:2), then we would know the stripes must be limited. Nobody would think for a moment that *any* punishment would last forever. Not even the lake of fire.

# PART 4

## Closing Thoughts on Calvinism and Arminianism

# 11

## Calvinist Conundrums

It is impossible to believe that "God is love" as the Apostle declares (1 John 4), and at the same time believe that he deliberately sat down to the work of giving existence to an immortal soul only that he might make that existence an endless curse to it. There can be no more awful blasphemy than this yoking together Infinite and Everlasting Love with Infinite and Everlasting Woe.

—THOMAS THAYER

IN THIS SECTION I wish to do two things; take a closer look at the Calvinist proof text Romans 9:22, which I have referenced throughout this book, and then explore a number of what I call "Calvinist Conundrums." In the preface I wrote:

> I am only asking the Calvinist to be consistent with his own theo-
> logical assertions. I am not trying to convince him that a good
> God doesn't torture people forever because it's *wrong* or that God's
> total sovereignty over the human will argues against eternal tor-
> ment because such a thing is *absurd and cruel*. No, I concede from
> the start that they accept that God, as far as the depraved human
> mind can see, operates in a way that *is* cruel and absurd. I will, of
> course, try to prove that they are wrong, but only by showing them
> their own scriptures and their own ideas demand it as a matter of
> logical consistency.

Part 4: **Closing Thoughts on Calvinism and Arminianism**

It is this task I will continue to pursue in my exploration of the Calvinist Conundrums.

## Romans 9:22

"What if God, willing to show his wrath, and to make his power known, endured with much longsuffering the vessels of wrath fitted to destruction: And that he might make known the riches of his glory on the vessels of mercy, which he had afore prepared unto glory."

I have already demonstrated the logical problems with employing this verse as a proof text. It leaves us with what I call *The Happy Coincidence* model of sin and salvation. That is:

1. From eternity past God intended that the most vivid and profound demonstration of His glory would come in the form of His work of salvation on the cross of Christ.

2. God then made man in order to punish him

3. He made him perfect, and thus unlikely to sin or ever need a savior

4. By a happy coincidence, and against all the odds, this perfect man sinned, thus allowing God to fulfill his purposes for both the man and Himself

5. When he sinned, God, who is now confronted with the prospect of being able to fulfill all of His original plans for both man and Christ, became *furious*

You don't need a degree from one of the theological cemeteries (where they bury truth) to see the problem in this system of thought. Any child could see it. But there's another, even more fundamental problem than the fact that we cannot build a coherent theology on this verse. It's the fact that the verse itself is taken out of context. The Calvinist takes this verse to mean God has elected some people to salvation and reprobated the rest. The elect will go to heaven and the reprobate to hell. Each group's fate has been fixed in the eternal counsels of God and can never be altered. This is what the Calvinists believe the verse is teaching. And the truth is that the verse—when taken alone—does seem to be teaching that very thing. But when taken in the context of Romans 9–11, it does not.

The Calvinist would have you believe that the thrust of these chapters is an assertion by Paul that God has a right to damn anyone he pleases.

Indeed Romans 9:18–19 states: "Therefore he hath mercy on whom he will have mercy, and whom he will he hardeneth. Thou wilt say then unto me, Why doth he yet find fault? For who hath resisted his will?"

What the Calvinist ignores is the context in which this question is raised. It is raised in regard to the Jew's jealousy over God including the Gentiles in his salvation plan. God is not saying "I will damn anyone I please"; he's saying "I will save anyone I please."[1] Chapter 11 goes on to make it clear that God intends to save *all* of Israel (verse 26) and that he "hath concluded all in unbelief, that he might have mercy upon all" (verse 32). Moreover, it is also clear that election takes place before a person is born (Romans 9:11). The Calvinist sees this as proof of God's "terrible decree," namely, that some are reprobated from eternity past. These chapters, however, suggest no such thing. Instead they are emphasizing two things:

1. that we are all players in a game that God has arranged, and

2. He is working it out to the good of all. This agrees entirely with Paul's message in Romans 8:20, that *God* subjected us to vanity with a plan to release us from it.

Romans 9:22 is a step in a plan of God's that culminates with "mercy upon all." It is not the plan in itself.

## Calvinist Conundrums

### Conundrum 1: Why shouldn't we believe God's real will is what He says it is?

Every theological system must develop a way of resolving the tension between disparate verses of scripture. Take for instance 1 Cor. 15:22: "As in Adam all die, so in Christ shall all be made alive." How do we reconcile this verse, which seems to promise salvation for all, with a verse like Rev. 14:11: "And the smoke of their torment ascendeth up forever and ever . . .," which seems to insist that only some will be saved? The Arminian, the Calvinist, and the Universalist will each offer a different explanation, one that will reconcile the verses in favor of their own particular system. But aside from the explanations, we must also explain why these contradictory verses exist

---

1. For a more complete treatment of this subject read chapter 7 of Thomas Talbott's *The Inescapable Love of God.*

in the first place. In other words, why did God so construct the bible so that some verses appear to teach one thing and others a different thing?

The Calvinists offer the explanation that God has a hidden will and a revealed will. The salvation verses suggest a revealed will to save all; the judgment verses suggest a hidden will to save only the elect. This concession on their part raises an obvious question, namely: What is stopping them from believing the reverse? What is stopping them from believing that God is hiding His will to save all men?

Simply consider the problems posed for Calvinism by the idea that God is hiding His will. First off, how does God hide the truth according to Calvinists? Remember, He is hiding the truth to *glorify Himself* (Proverbs 25:2). We would expect, therefore, that He employs a method suited to this goal. What ingenious method does the infinite mind of God employ to conceal the full import of His revelation to the puny mind of man? Well, in a word: wordplay. He comes announcing the "good news" to "all men," and declaring Himself to be the savior of "the world." He declares that He's tasted death for "every man," and justified "all" men, that He wills that "all men" be saved and that "none perish" and that "every tongue" confess Him as Lord, and that all things be subjected to Himself, and that all creation be set free, and that all who died in Adam be made alive in Christ.

But does He mean any of it? According to the Calvinists, no. Apparently, here is where the genius of God comes into play. He does indeed say all of those things; that much is understood. But He also employs a brilliant plan, one which only divine Omniscience could conceive, by which all of those words are negated and rendered meaningless. He sprinkles throughout scripture words like "all" and "every" in ways that do not necessarily include all men. In other words, He often employs those phrases in a limited sense, thereby inoculating Himself against any charge of deceit should one claim that the word "all" in Romans 5:18 or 1 Cor. 15:22 really ought to mean all without exception.

But that's only a sample of His genius. He also hides the truth by making it appear inconsistent, not only with His promises, but with no less than four other things:

1. God's revealed character in Christ

God is love (1 John 4:8)

2. Reason and conscience (as *affirmed* by scripture)

"If ye then, being evil, know how to give good gifts unto your children, how much more shall your Father which is in heaven give good things to them that ask him?" (Luke 11:13)

### 3. God's laws regarding the extent and purpose of punishment

"For the Lord will not cast off forever: But though he cause grief, yet he will have compassion according to the multitude of his mercies. For he does not afflict willingly nor grieve the children of men. (Lamentations 3:32–33)

"No chastening for the present seemeth to be joyous, but grievous: nevertheless afterward it yieldeth the peaceable fruit of righteousness unto those which are exercised thereby." (Hebrews 2:11)

"Forty stripes he may give him, and not exceed . . ." (Deuteronomy 25:3)

"For he knows our frame; he remembers that we are but dust." (Psalm 103:14)

### 4. The biblically affirmed fact that God is the father of all men

You are our Father . . . our potter; and all we are the work of Your hand (Is. 64:8).

Have we not all one Father? Has not one God created us (Mal. 2:10)?

Leave it to the ingenious mind of God to set His laws, promises, character, and man's reason against His own will in such a way as to conceal that will from the masses. Yes, this is how the Calvinist believes God glorifies Himself. By concealing something from men by the same kind of methods a *man* might employ to conceal things from other men. Methods that amount to nothing more than wordplay and deceit. And the most pedestrian form of it at that. That brings glory to the God of the Universe?

Let us take a moment to consider the implications involved in the idea of God hiding the truth. The very notion forces us to ask a very important question: Is God a better concealer than we are detectives? Of course to ask the question is to answer it. We must admit, therefore, that we cannot discover the truth simply by reading the bible. God must reveal it to us. It is impossible to overestimate the importance of this fact. It means we cannot know we have come to truth simply because we have found an amicable way of putting scripture together. There are dozens of such ways. If God is out to fool us, then surely He can lead us into a *false* way of putting scripture together.

So, then how do we know we are coming to truth? There's only one way: by the witness of the Spirit. But how do we know it's leading us into truth and not error? I would suggest a simple test. The bible says "The truth shall set you free" (Jn. 8:32). What does that mean? It means the truth will lead us out of darkness into light. It will answer questions rather than raising a host of new ones. It will lessen mystery rather than deepen it. If it's not doing these things, then what reason do we have for believing that it's truth? Because it's what the bible says? The bible—which *hides* truth?

The Calvinist, of course, must reject this form of thinking for the obvious reason. The Calvinist experience of "truth" leads to deeper darkness. It raises dozens of logical impossibilities (which we will enumerate in this section). Reason must be twisted beyond recognition to accommodate the "truth" of the Calvinist system. The Calvinist truth leads them into impenetrable darkness. It leads them into truth which looks *exactly like a lie*. But they know it's truth because the bible, *which hides truth*, says so!

The bible says to "try the spirits whether they are from God." A Spirit of truth will lead us into truth, not lies; into light, not darkness. Otherwise the scripture is fulfilled in us which says "If therefore the light that is in thee be darkness, how great is that darkness" (Mt. 6:23)!

## Conundrum 2: Why not apply God's hidden will to Adam?

Calvinists understand God's will by working backwards from what they believe the results will be. In other words, if people go to hell, then God wants people to go to hell. It's a simple formula:

A. Men go to hell, therefore

B. God wants men to go to hell

And yet notice something very curious. They do not apply this same logic to the Adam story. They do not say:

A. Adam sinned, therefore

B. God wanted Adam to sin

They have decided, in the case of man's eternal destiny, to infer God's will based on circumstantial evidence. In other words, God's revealed will—that all be saved—contradicts the evidence; therefore we must conclude that His revealed will is not His real will; His hidden will is His real will. And yet when it comes to the case of Adam, they take the exact opposite approach. They ignore the overwhelming circumstantial evidence that God's hidden will was for Adam to eat the fruit of the tree, and insist that His revealed will—that Adam not eat the fruit—was His real will. And they take this stance despite the fact that, as we have seen, God would have told Adam not to eat from the tree *even had He wanted him to do so.*

Moreover, to infer that God does not want all men to be saved requires a denial of positive statements of scripture, whereas to assert that God wanted Adam to sin requires only that we remove Satan from the picture in *exactly the same way* Job did when he attributed all of his affliction to God—after which God said that Job spoke rightly and his friends did not (Job 42:7). If ever there was a *need* to infer a hidden will, it was here. And that's not to mention the positive declaration of Rom. 8:20 that *God* subjected creation to vanity, *not willingly.* The following tables illustrate the difference in perspectives between the Calvinists and Universalists.

### Calvinists

| | Revealed Will | Hidden or "Real" Will | Reason for Choice |
|---|---|---|---|
| **Adam** | That Adam not eat the apple | That Adam not eat the apple | Revealed will wins because God cannot tempt man; God made man perfect |
| **Man in general** | That all men be saved | That most men be damned | Hidden will wins because many verses indicate man will be damned; therefore it is God's will. Verses implying universal salvation (in accordance with revealed will) must be understood in light of God's hidden will to save only some |

### Universalist

| | Revealed Will | Hidden or "real" Will | Reason for Choice |
|---|---|---|---|
| **Adam** | That Adam not eat the apple | That Adam eat the apple | The command would have been the same either way; therefore, we must look to the circumstantial evidence to determine intent. All circumstantial evidence points to fact that God wanted Adam to eat the apple. |

| **Man in general** | That all men be saved | That all men be saved | God created man in His own image (Gen. 1:27, 9:6) |
|---|---|---|---|

He is the father of all men (Ps. 82:6; Is. 64:8, Mal. 2:10, Mt. 6:9, 23:1,9, Acts 17:22, 28–29, Ep. 3:14–15, Heb. 12:9)

He did not create us with free will. We respond to causes that He set in motion; hence our actions could not have been otherwise (Romans 9:19). This is inconsistent with eternal torment.

Christ was not eternally tormented; hence if any man should have to bear that punishment it will mean God is exacting a greater punishment than that which is necessary by law to atone for sin

He wills that all be saved (1 Tim. 2:4)

He died for every man (Heb. 2:9)

The bible contains many verses that anyone of normal understanding would take to suggest Universal Salvation (Phil 2:10, Col. 1:15–20), Rom. 5:18, 1 Cor. 15:22, Eph 1:10)

God never promised to send anyone to hell

A promise cannot be annulled by a threat; in the event of a scriptural stalemate, the promise wins (Gal. 3:17)

The bible records many instances of eternal punishments that were not, in fact, eternal (Deut. 23:3; Ezra 10:2,3,44; Neh. 13:1, 23, 25, 30; Jer. 48:42; Ezek. 21:28, 32; Jer. 48:47; 49:6; Isa. 19:21,25; Jude 1:7, Ezek. 16:53, 55)

To maintain a doctrine of eternal torment we must admit that God's plan runs contrary to His revealed character in Christ, our God-given reason and conscience, His own laws (Mt. 8:22, Luke 11:13, 15:4, James 3:7, 1 Tim. 5:21, Deut. 23:22, Mal. 2:16) and His promises.

Our origin indicates our destiny. The bible says we were all created in, for, and by Christ, and that we are all going back to Him in the end (Col. 1:16; Rom. 11:36)

## Conundrum 3: Infinite sin contradicts degrees of punishment

Most Calvinists believe that the bible teaches degrees of punishment in hell. This idea, however, contradicts their justification for eternal punishment in the first place. The Calvinist reasons that we deserve eternal punishment by virtue of the fact that our sin is committed against an infinite God. The problem with this reasoning is obvious: if the punishment is based not on the gravity of the offense, but on the majesty of the One offended, then all sins—even the smallest—deserve equal punishment; hence there could be no degrees of punishment in hell. It also violates the scriptures, which insist God does consider our own inherent weaknesses when assessing penalties. "He is mindful of our frame, that we are dust." (Psalm 103:14)

## Conundrum 4: The Infinite Majesty defense doesn't wash

Calvinists defend infinite punishment based on the Infinite Majesty of God theory. The transgression is measured by the greatness of the one offended; hence, when we offend infinite God, we deserve infinite punishment. But they overlook a very obvious fact: God can hate sin infinitely and *not* be infinitely offended by it. How can this be?

On the contrary, how can it not be? Yes, God, as a perfectly pure being, can have no darkness in Him. But does this perfect purity mean that He must be infinitely offended when an *imperfect* creature sins? Why would it? I can *hate* violence completely and absolutely and yet not be terribly *offended* by certain acts of violence. For instance, a two year old child's violent temper tantrum does not offend me at all. An eight year old's tantrum would offend me more, and a grown man's still more. But even in the case of grown men, there are gradations of offense based on the mental capacity and overall wellness of the offender. I can despise the particular offense absolutely and yet not be absolutely offended by it in each and every instance. Hatred of violence does not translate proportionally into hatred of the perpetrator of every violent act. It's absurd to imagine that the only factor God considers in accessing the penalty for sin is His own nature. Does God not realize that His *own* inability to sin is a product of this nature? And that He has *not* conferred upon man this same nature? Are we really to propose that God is ignorant of this fact? If so, then why does the bible *affirm* this very thing, insisting that the *natural* man is under the *law* of sin and death, and *cannot* obey God's commands, while also insisting that the spiritual man *cannot* sin? (Rom. 8:2,8; 1 Jn. 3:9) And why does it very clearly emphasize that Adam and Christ were made *differently*? (1 Cor. 15:44)

## Conundrum 5: There's no need for ongoing sin—and therefore ongoing punishment—in hell

Another common argument for the necessity of eternal punishment is that sin will continue in hell; therefore the punishment will continue to mount accordingly. The very premise is deeply flawed. Thomas Allin writes: "It is usually alleged that there will be an endless continuance of sinning, with probably an endless aggravation, and therefore the punishment must be endless. Is not this like an admission of disproportion between the punishment and the original cause of its infliction?"[2]

But even if we accept the premise that all sin—even in hell—must be punished, we need not accept the necessity of eternal punishment. This argument tacitly acknowledges that man's guilt upon first entering hell is finite and that if no more were incurred, he could expect the punishment to terminate. Could God arrange such a scenario? Of course he could. He need only to so intensify the punishment that the sinner would be completely unable to sin. How could He do this? How could He punish in a way so as to preclude all sin, even in thought? Simple. He can fully immerse the person in a vat of molten lava, thus inflicting a pain so intense that it would render all thought impossible. In this manner the sinner endures his punishment without incurring anymore. God could retain him in this state until such time as His wrath is fully satisfied, after which he could either annihilate or—better yet—save the person.

Or,

He could save the person while he's actually in hell. That way he will endure his punishment with the same mindset that Christ endured His—without sinning.

## Conundrum 6: Hell is not necessary to satisfy God's justice

Calvinists generally operate on the belief in Christ's substitutionary atonement. Christ's death appeased the Father's wrath, thus serving as a propitiation for sins. According to this theory, Christ became sin on the cross, God punished our sin in Him, and opened the way for God to forgive us. By this logic, there is simply no need for God to demonstrate his wrath by sending anyone to hell. He could have just as amply demonstrated that wrath by saving all men. Randall Rauser writes:

2. Allin et al., *Christ Triumphant* ch 10.

"An elect person has the full righteousness of Christ imputed to him or her. Christ has fully satisfied the wrath and justice of God on the cross and since that elect individual is counted in Christ that individual is a complete token of the infinite justice."

By contrast,

A reprobate individual must suffer eternally to satisfy the demands of justice apart from the imputed righteousness of Christ. Since it is impossible to traverse an actual infinite series of temporal moments it is impossible for this reprobate individual ever to satisfy fully the demands of divine justice and thereby become a complete token of that infinite justice.

To sum up, the Calvinist is proposing that a possible world in which divine justice is perfectly satisfied in some and only potentially satisfied in others is more illustrative of divine justice than a world in which divine justice is satisfied in all. But this is clearly false. To provide an analogy, that is like claiming that 500 infinite deposits into a bank account coupled with 500 finite deposits is worth more than a 1000 infinite deposits.

Consequently, the consistent Calvinist will either embrace universal salvation or reject Calvinist election.[3]

## Conundrum 7: The Just Desserts defense doesn't wash

A major tenet of Calvinism is that God reprobates the non-elect in order to demonstrate his justice in punishing them. This is not unjust, the Calvinist argues, due to the fact that they are only getting what they deserve. God, therefore, created the non-elect in order that they might commit sins deserving of eternal punishment. This seems to let God off the hook; after all, how can you argue with justice? The punishment must fit the crime, right? It does, however, raise another question: Did God have a moral obligation to prevent us from ever incurring such a *deserved* punishment?

Suppose a psychiatrist is treating a patient. The patient is exhibiting certain behaviors which, if unchecked, will surely lead him to harm himself. The psychiatrist, however, does not prescribe any medicine, instead reasoning that the man will deserve whatever harm befalls him. Let's further suppose that the psychiatrist is totally correct in his assessment; the man will indeed harm himself and will indeed deserve it. Would his failure to prescribe the medicine be justifiable by any conceivable standards of

3. Rauser, "Why Calvinists should be Universalists or Armenians."

decency? If anything, allowing the man to plunge himself into a *deserved* ruin is even *worse*, for then he is allowing the man's total destruction—body and soul—when he could have easily prevented it.

And yet the Calvinist God is even worse than that. He is not merely administering a just penalty after the fact; He is deliberately arranging circumstances in order that a person will come to deserve a terrible penalty. Worse still, He *creates* a person for that very purpose. In order to deserve any punishment at all, a person must first exist. We don't deserve *anything* before we are born. What did anyone do to *deserve* being forced into existence in order to incur eternal punishment?

## Conundrum 8: The Total Depravity defense doesn't wash

The Calvinist tells us we cannot understand things. Depravity has corrupted our moral senses. My inner moral conviction that it's wrong for God to eternally torment his own creatures cannot be trusted. But why should I believe depravity has corrupted my own inner moral convictions more than it has corrupted *the way Calvinists interpret the bible*?

## Conundrum 9: Calvinists use their own despised reason to arrive at their conclusions

Mark 3:22 says it's an unpardonable sin to attribute to God the works of the devil. It behooves us, therefore, to pay particular attention to what God takes credit for, and what He doesn't, lest we attribute to the devil the works of God. Isaiah 45:7 says: "I form the light, and create darkness: I make peace, and create evil: I the Lord do all these things." Has the Christian religious system, by insisting that man created evil, committed the offense discussed in Mark 3:22? Have they ascribed to the devil the work of God? The Calvinist, who knows man does not have free will, and believe God *made* man for sin, nevertheless insists on blaming man. Why? Because God could not create evil? No. Because He *wouldn't*. But why does he say this, in spite of what God's own word says? Because he believes such a thing is impossible. He uses his *reason* to absolve God. He uses his own puny, finite mind to dictate how God is supposed to behave. This is the very thing Calvinists insist we *must never do*.

Conundrum 10: The Calvinist conception of sin ought to remove any need to absolve God of it

On both the Calvinist and the Universalist models, God allows sin for the purpose of a fuller expression and demonstration than might have occurred without it. On the Calvinist model, the sin is permitted for God's glory in punishing it; on the Universalist model it is allowed for God's glory in defeating it and, in the process, instilling certain lessons and experiences to mankind. The reason, I believe, that the Calvinist opts for their model is that the Universalist model makes God complicit in sin. On the Universalist model God—in a sense—creates evil for the ultimate good of man. On the Calvinist model, God has no complicity in evil. He simply allows it and then deals with it in a way that most enhances his glory.

But this raises a problem. Generally we define sin against man as sin against God, in keeping with Proverbs 14:31. This model, however, cannot apply in Calvinism. God does not love everyone; hence sin against man, *per se*, does not offend Him. In other words the fact that Sam punches Sally in the nose for no particular reason does not really offend God. At least not for the reason we would think, namely, that Sally was hurt, and God felt bad for her. The Calvinist God, by definition, cannot feel this way. The Calvinist God is totally sovereign; if He loved Sally, He would save her. The fact that He doesn't means he doesn't love her; hence he could hardly be offended by the fact that someone hurt her. The offense consists not in the fact that we sin against each other, but in the fact that we offend *Him*. But if sin consists not in hurting each other, but in hurting Him, then by allowing sin God is only complicit in *allowing Himself to be harmed*. And is *that* really a sin? Especially if it's done with a good intent for the one committing the harm? If I allow you to hurt me in order to help you, have I really committed a sin? The Calvinist definition of sin renders sin not sinful; therefore there should be no *need* to absolve Him of it.

If, however, we allow that sin is what the *bible* says it is, which is sin against man (Prov. 14:31), then we have a God who can only be offended by sin because He loves the sinner. And you can't hate the sin *more* than you love the sinner when the one (hatred of sin) stems from the other (love of the sinner). Moreover, the love for the sinner must come *before* the hatred of the sin. The hatred of the sin exists only as a corollary to the love of the sinner. Either God hates sin because He loves the sinner, in which case the love must be stronger than the hate, or He hates because He is offended, in which case He is the only injured party; hence no harm has been permitted to anyone else, except as *meaningless collateral damage*, and thus He has not been complicit in allowing anyone to be harmed other than Himself; therefore He is not really complicit in sin by any rational understanding of the concept.

The Calvinist, therefore, by going against the bible definition of sin, has actually rendered the meaning of sin such as to preclude the possibility of any meaningful complicity on God's part.

## Conundrum 11: Love is inclusive

Thomas Talbott writes:

> "Indeed, if we say that we love God whilst hating some of our brothers and sisters, then we are liars. But the reverse is true as well: Just as we cannot love God and hate those whom He loves, neither can God love us and, at the same time hate those whom we love. If I truly love my daughter *as myself*, then God cannot love (or will the good for me) unless He also loves (or wills the good for) her . . .
>
> "So as long as I love my daughter *as myself*, then God cannot truly love me without loving my daughter as well. An additional point is this: So long as I love my daughter as myself, I can neither love God nor worship him unless I at least *believe* that he loves my daughter as well; the idea that I could *both* love my daughter *and* love a God whom I know to hate her is also logically absurd. For consider what my love for God would have to entail: It would entail, first, that I respect God and approve of his actions, second, that I am grateful to God for what he has done for me, and third, that my will is, on the important issues at least, in conformity with his. But if I truly love my daughter, desiring the good for her, and God does not, then (a) my will is *not* in conformity with God's, (b) I could not consistently approve of God's attitude towards my daughter, and © neither could I be grateful to him for the harm he is doing to me . . . As a matter of logic, either I do not love my daughter *as myself*, or I do not love God with all my heart, or I do not believe that God himself fails to love my own daughter."[4]

4. Talbott, *The Inescapable Love of God*, 140.

## Conundrum 12: Calvinism violates rules of sound bible interpretation

Calvinism renders the whole bible a sham. Just a sampling of some of the verses that must be butchered to accommodate their doctrine:

> God is love (1 Jn. 4:8) really means this: God is part love and part hate.
>
> God is light (1 Jn. 1:15) really means this: God is part light and part darkness.
>
> He desires that none perish (2 Peter 3:9) really means this: He desires that most perish.
>
> Love thy neighbor as thyself (Luke 10:27) really means this: Love your neighbor and the God you believe hates them.

And so on.

Thomas Allin writes:

> When they say *all* men, I assume them to mean all men. When they speak of all things, I assume them to mean *all* things. When they speak of life and salvation as given to the world, I assume them to mean *given* and not merely offered. When they speak of the destruction of death, of the devil, and of the works of the devil, I assume them to mean that these shall be *destroyed* and not preserved forever in hell. When they tell us the whole of Creation suffers but that it shall be delivered, I assume that they mean the actual deliverance of all created things. When they tell us that Redemption is wider, broader, and stronger than the Fall, I assume that they mean to tell us at least this, that *all* the evil caused by the Fall shall be swept away. When they describe Christ's empire as extending over all things and all creatures, and tell us that every tongue must join in homage to Him, I assume them to mean what these words convey in their ordinary sense. If I did not, should I not be making God a liar?"[5]

## Conundrum 13: Calvinism renders God a law unto Himself

Calvinists believe that God's will is a law unto itself, whereby a thing is right because God says so, regardless of what that thing involves. Psalm

---

5. Allin et al., *Christ Triumphant* ch 8.

138:2, however, indicates exactly the opposite; "I will worship toward thy holy temple, and praise thy name for thy lovingkindness and for thy truth: for thou hast magnified thy word above all thy name." God's word is above his name. He follows His own law, acting out of a moral sense of right and wrong. In other words, it's not right because God says so; God says so because it's right.

## Conundrum 14: The Calvinist God is no better than men

If God's more concerned with His glory than my happiness, then why am I wrong to be more concerned with my happiness than His glory? Is He not just as selfish as I am?

## Conundrum 15: Necessary evils are not forever

Thomas Thayer wrote:

> For aught we know, God may have created somewhere in infinite space a world without evil, peopled by a race of beings morally perfect. But even if this were so, it would remain to be proved that *this* world, and man as we find him here, imperfect and subject to evil, do not constitute a link in the endless chain of being, without which it would be incomplete . . .[6]

It is a common theme among Universalist authors—the idea that God probably had good reason to make man imperfect and liable to sin. The best of all possible worlds (henceforth I will call it BOAP), according to the Universalist, is one that probably includes sin. What's fascinating is that the Calvinist fully agrees with this assertion. In fact, it is the very cornerstone of Calvinist theology. The Calvinist believes that the BOAP is one in which God maximally displays all of His attributes. Justice is one of those attributes. God, therefore, had to create vessels of wrath in order to punish as a display of His justice. It is apparent then that both camps accept the idea that the BOAP includes sin. Then why do Universalist authors bother to make this point? One that does nothing to rebut their opponents? Do they labor in vein?

I don't think so. What we have here are two camps doing different dances to the same music. But only one camp is actually dancing in

6. Thayer, *Theology of Universalism*, 16.

*harmony* to that music. The point in question *does* argue against Calvinism. I will demonstrate how. Let us accept the proposition that God wishes to maximally display all of His attributes. Let us further suppose that God never planned to send a single soul to hell. Would God have *still* have had to create man imperfect in order to maximally display His attributes? Could a perfect, pristine universe, untouched by corruption of any kind, have afforded God the opportunity to maximally display His glory to His creatures? And is it likely that He would have *wanted* to display that glory simply by creating men perfect and instilling in us, at the moment of our conception, all that pertains to happiness and holiness?

If the answer to either of these questions is no, then the Calvinists have a dilemma on their hands. God, in order to maximally display His glory, had to make man imperfect *even if He never planned to send a single soul to hell.* Then why, when a perfectly good motive naturally exists for making man imperfect, would they want to ascribe to Him such a perfectly *awful* motive? Indeed it is the very fact that God wishes to maximally display His attributes that all but dictates that He would not create man perfect, for such a method does not really permit much of a *display* at all; rather it involves an *imparting*, as one might impart knowledge into a computer by the insertion of a chip. And so the *very motive the Calvinist employ to suggest that God made us for hell*—His need to maximally display His attributes—is the *very same thing* that makes it extremely unlikely that He would have made us perfect from the start. We can plainly see, therefore, that the very foundation of Calvinist thought—the idea that if sin exists it can only be in order to punish it—entails a positively stupefying travesty of logic.

The fact is that God, in order to display His attributes, had to create, not sin and punishment, as the Calvinists insist, but corruption and vanity, as the bible insists. His strength is perfected in ... what? *Weakness.* (2 Cor. 12:9) And how was man created? ". . it is sown in weakness . . ." (1 Cor. 15:43) In other words, God had to create for man an environment where the attributes of Christ could flourish. The bible never says that God's goal in creation was sin and punishment. In fact, it expressly denies this: "Let no man say when he is tempted, I am tempted of God . . ." and " . . . 'As I live,' says the Lord God, 'I have no pleasure in the death of the wicked, but that the wicked turn from his way and live.'" (Ezek. 33:11) This is where we must rightly divide the word of truth. The Calvinist would have us believe God created man perfect, and yet in order to sin. The truth is just the opposite:

He created us imperfect, but not for the *purpose* of sinning. Here's what the bible says:

> "For the creature was made subject to vanity, not willingly, but by reason of him who hath subjected the same, in hope, Because the creature itself also shall be delivered from the bondage of corruption into the glorious liberty of the children of God."

Man's imperfect nature allows for a demonstration that would have otherwise been impossible. To reduce this demonstration to nothing more than God's mercy, as shown in vessels of mercy, and justice, as shown in vessels of wrath, is incredibly simplistic and fails to consider the broader picture. There are *many* things on display in this world besides mercy and punishment. What about contrast? The chance to observe and experience the *difference* between things? Did not Adam eat from a tree whose fruit contained the knowledge of *both* good and evil? And what about Christ Himself? Hebrews 8:5 says even Christ "learned obedience by things which he suffered." How could He have suffered anything in a world without evil? And so it is with all men. We must suffer. God did not make us perfect, and yet for sin and punishment. He made us imperfect in order to learn obedience by the things we suffer.

But of course all of this is mere conjecture if the scripture does not back it up. Does it? Quite explicitly. 1 Cor. 15:46 states the matter clearly and concisely: "Howbeit that was not first which was spiritual, but that which is natural; and afterward that which is spiritual." There is a natural growth process. It is from the natural to the spiritual. It's called *development*, and you can't have it by making man perfect from the start. If anyone would suggest that the word *natural* does not denote evil of any kind, I would merely refer them to the subsequent verses.

> "So also is the resurrection of the dead. It is sown in corruption; it is raised in incorruption: It is sown in dishonour; it is raised in glory; it is sown in weakness; it is raised in power: It is sown a natural body; it is raised a spiritual body. There is a natural body, and there is a spiritual body. And so it is written, The first man Adam was made a living soul; the last Adam was made a quickening spirit."

These verses give the lie to the Arminian idea that corruption is an unwanted intruder into God's holy universe, and to the Calvinist idea that it was created as an end in itself. This was God's plan of creation; it was not an accommodation to unwanted events, as the Arminians would suggest; nor was it enacted with malice, as the Calvinists suggest. It is simply the way God ordained that things would proceed—by stages. It is exactly the way we would *expect* a perfect Creator to create.

## Conundrum 16: You can't blame man if it's God's will

It is impossible to assert, as the Calvinists do, that God made us to punish us, and yet then also assert that the reason for our punishment is our own sin. If God makes us for punishment, then sin is not the reason for punishment; His will is. Our sin is the *pretext*. This is easy to illustrate. Everyone knows about the flinch game. You make a person flinch, then give him two punches for flinching. What is the cause of the punching? The flinching? Or the desire of one person to punch the other person? Of course it is the desire of one person to punch the other. The flinching is the *pretext* for the punching. The smallest child can understand this. And yet the Calvinist does not. He insists that God made man for punishment, yet man's sin is the cause, not God's will to punish.

## Conundrum 17: The Calvinist God should be thanking us for sin

The Calvinist God simply has no reason to get angry at all. According to the Calvinist, God made man for wrath. He made him in order to provide the fullest demonstration of both His mercy in saving man from sin, and His wrath in punishing him for it. The Calvinist God, therefore, ought to be *happy* that man sinned. The Calvinist position furnishes us with the most logically improbable theological system ever conceived by the mind of man. It is what I call *The Happy Coincidence* model of sin and salvation. That is:

1. From eternity past God intended that the most vivid and profound demonstration of his glory would come in the form of his work of salvation on the cross of Christ.

2. God then made man in order to punish him

3. He made him perfect, and thus unlikely to ever sin or need a savior

4. By a happy coincidence, and against all the odds, this perfect man sinned, thus allowing God to fulfill his purposes for both the man and Himself

5. When he sinned, God, who is now confronted with the prospect of being able to fulfill all of His original plans for both man and Christ, became *furious*

You don't need a degree from one of the theological cemeteries (where they bury truth) to see the problem in this system of thought. Any child could see that it is an incoherent hodgepodge of tortured logic.

## Conundrum 18: The Calvinist is trying to separate that which God has joined

The Calvinist and the Universalist each employ their own proof text as to why man was created. The Calvinist employs Romans 9:22; the Universalist Romans 8:20.

> Romans 9:22–23: "What if God, willing to show his wrath, and to make his power known, endured with much longsuffering the vessels of wrath fitted to destruction: And that he might make known the riches of his glory on the vessels of mercy, which he had afore prepared unto glory."

> Romans 8:20–21: "For the creature was made subject to vanity, not willingly, but by reason of him who hath subjected the same, in hope, Because the creature itself also shall be delivered from the bondage of corruption into the glorious liberty of the children of God."

I will now demonstrate that the Calvinist, if he is consistent, must agree with Rom 8:20, while disagreeing with Romans 8:21.

The Calvinist believes that in the best of all possible worlds, sin must exist. It must exist because, as Romans 9:22 insists, God must display his glory by punishing it. But if the best of all possible worlds includes sin, then God had to create man not only liable to sin, but *certain* to sin. He had to "make man subject to vanity." But notice the problem. Romans 8:20 insists that God subjected creation to vanity, not, as the Calvinist insists, to punish him for it, but rather to *free* him from it. Vanity was not created as an end in itself, but as a means to an end. And to this the scriptures agree:

> "Howbeit that was not first which is spiritual, but that which is natural; and afterward that which is spiritual." (1 Cor 15:46)

> "For the Lord will not cast off forever: But though he cause grief, yet he will have compassion according to the multitude of his

mercies. For he does not afflict willingly nor grieve the children of men. (Lamentations 3:32–33)

"It is an experience of evil Elohim [God] has given to the sons of humanity to humble them by it." (Concordant Old Testament)

But Calvinist theology attributes to God an entirely different motive in giving us an "experience of evil"—and an unspeakably fiendish one at that. Calvinist theology, therefore, would require that they render Romans 8:20–21 this way: "For the creature was made subject to vanity, not willingly, but by reason of him who hath subjected the same, in order to torment them forever in hell." The Calvinist simply cannot establish a logical link between the *way* God made us and the *why*. On the one hand, they insist He made us to punish us, which, to any rationale mind, would mean He made us "subject to vanity"; on the other hand, they insist He made us perfect. All Romans 8:20 does is insist on a logical link between the *way* God made us and the *why*.

The Calvinist might raise the objection that he does not believe this verse applies to human beings. No matter. According to his own theology it *does* apply to human beings—at least the first half. His God *had* to make man subject to vanity in order to fulfill His own purposes. We therefore have a verse that perfectly describes the way the Calvinist God *had* to create man, which they say doesn't apply to man because they don't like the next verse!

## Conundrum 19: The Calvinist God is actually pretty pathetic

There is something incredibly demeaning about having to force existence upon someone, suit them with a defective nature, then get them to behave in a certain deplorable manner so that you might punish them for your own personal glory. Isn't wrenching someone out of the peaceful repose of non-existence in order to punish them to show your justice an inherent contradiction? Isn't there something pathetic about it?

## Conundrum 20: Calvinism denies the nature of truth

We save the best for last. It's the best because it works as a rebuttal for Calvinism *and* Arminianism. John 8:32 says "The truth will set you free." It always seemed to me that Calvinism denied this basic truth. The truth, according to them, is a good thing for some and a horrible thing for others. God loves some people and hates others. The truth for some people is that God hates them. But how can this be? If the truth sets us free, then the truth—for all people—must be something liberating. The Calvinist might respond along the following lines: Only the elect will ever know the truth. This truth will set *them* free. The rest are blinded. The problem with this response is that it only considers one half of the equation—the elect. It ignores the other half. What about the ones being blinded? The ones God hates. Suppose I'm one of the ones God hates. How would knowing that God hates me set me free? Mark 4:12–15 says that God blinds people to keep them from seeing the truth and repenting. What truth is being concealed? The truth that God hates me? How could this be? If the truth being concealed is something that would set me free, then how can it be something bad? The truth must be something *good*. How could concealing the fact that God hates me prevent me from repenting?

Perhaps the Calvinist could respond as follows: You're not being blinded to the fact that God loves you; He may love you and He may not. The nature of the blindness is something else. You are being blinded to the nature of sin; you don't see how self-defeating it really is, and therefore you keep sinning. If you knew the truth—that sin is useless—it would set you free.

But that will not do either. Knowing the truth about sin doesn't produce repentance unless there's something to *replace* the sin with. That something must be a relationship with God. Suppose God gave me a perfect revelation about the nature of sin—one that dispelled all of my illusions about it. Now further suppose that along with *that* truth, He also shared with me another truth—the truth that He hates me. Will I repent? What causes repentance in the elect? Is it an understanding of the nature of sin or an assurance that God loves them? Moreover, if He doesn't love me, and my sin is due in large part to this fact, then I am not sinning due to any illusions; I am sinning due to a correct understanding about the nature of my relationship with God. I have no comfort in God; therefore I seek it by the only means available—sin. I am in fact acting in perfect accordance with the truth.

A big part of the reason we sin is *fear*. Hebrews 2:15 says we are enslaved to our sin due to our fear of death. Sin can only be removed by removing fear: Perfect love casts out fear (1 Jn. 4:18). If God hates me, and I know it, then I *already have the truth, and the truth is keeping me enslaved.* If God *might* love me, but might not, and I know it, then I have the truth and the truth is keeping me enslaved. The only possible way God could keep me in bondage by concealing the truth is if the truth were something that would *set me free from the bondage.*

Five point Calvinist Harold Camping writes: "God is so righteous that even the smallest sin is sufficient to cause a person to be eternally damned."[7] He also makes clear that "Christ is the Savior only to those who were given to him by the Father" and did not "lay down his life for every individual" or even pray for them. And yet he says:

> "If God plans to save us, He will do so in His own time . . . Wonderfully, God gives us much comfort by the promise of Philippians 4:6: "Be careful [anxious] for nothing; but in every thing by prayer and supplication with thanksgiving let your requests be known unto God." . . . Thus God is comforting us to rest entirely in Him. He is encouraging us to tell Him all about our anxiety. Marvelously, He is absolutely faithful and trustworthy to do His perfect will."[8]

Translation: *God, who doesn't love you, didn't die for you, and doesn't pray for you, and who is poised to eternally damn you for the smallest sin, is imploring you to lay aside your anxiety and rest in the assurance that His will is always done.* This is not a parody of the Calvinist position; it is exactly what their beliefs dictate; hence the need for the layers of circumvention and double-talk in their writings and teachings. No wonder the Orthodox Christian teaching is seen as such a joke by the secular man. It is presented as a joke by the Christians themselves. George Carlin put it this way: "There's a big man in the sky, whose watching what you do with your hands, and He has these ten things that He doesn't want you to do, and if you do them you'll burn forever, *but he loves you.*" Camping would have left out the last part, but the rest is pretty much right on the money.

Fortunately, there's a much better answer available to the unsaved man. Here's what Camping should have said: *You may not be saved. Perhaps you are indeed being blinded to the truth. But if this is indeed your unfortunate plight, you can rest assured that it is not because God doesn't love you. It's because He's blinding you to the fact that He does. Wonderfully, this veil will one day be lifted and you too, along with all of creation, will be set free from your subjection to sin and death.*

---

7. Camping, *I Hope God Will Save Me,* 55.

8. Camping, *God's Magnificent Salvation Plan,* 41–42.

Sadly, the the Calvinists not only deny that the truth will set you free; they construct a scenario whereby the *lie* sets you free. Even the Calvinist understands the difficulty in loving a God who hates you, and most—if not all—Calvinists become Calvinists only *after* coming to faith in Christ. Therefore, they posit the idea that we first come to God believing that He loves all, then, after we are saved, we understand that this is not really the case. In other words, we come to the truth (God loves me) by first believing a lie (God loves everyone).

This argument works equally well against Arminianism. John 8:32 insists that a clear vision of God is certain to produce repentance. The common perception is that God must take heroic measures to save us by wrestling our evil wills into conformity with His own. The truth is just the opposite: He must, in point of fact, take heroic measures to *keep us* from repenting (Mark 4:12). Anyone who sees God as he *truly* is will repent. 1 John 3:2 states: " . . . we shall be like him; *for we* shall see him *as he is.*" It doesn't say we will be like Him *and* we will see Him as He is; it says *for.* Cause and effect. Seeing the truth *will* produce repentance.

Shirley C. Guthrie writes:

> "Logically, evil is impossible in a world created and ruled by God, for it is just what God did *not* create and does *not* will. This is the parasitical power of evil. It is not the truth about who we are and what the world is like; it is a *lie*, a *contradiction*, and *denial* of the truth . . . Evil is the Big Lie that is so destructive and terrible just because it convinces us that the truth about God, God's world, and life in it is not the truth."[9]

How appropriate that this quote is from a book entitled Christian Doctrine. It's appropriate because this silliness *is* Christian Doctrine. He starts off with two lies, namely that evil is just what God did *not* create and does *not* will. What does the scripture say?

"I create evil" (Isa. 45:7)

"He hath . . . formed the crooked serpent" (Job 26:13)

"I have created the Waster to destroy" (Isa. 54:16)

Then he goes on to say, in effect, that evil has no life of it's own; it's only a result of ignorance. "It is *not who we are.*" And yet, we are to believe that God will keep us trapped forever in a state of existence that *is not who we*

---

9. Guthrie, *Christian Doctrine*, 188.

*are*, in order to punish us for *being in that state*. Can we conceive of a more grotesque form of injustice than to punish someone who is in a condition that in no way reflects who they really are? Make no mistake; this is not a caricature of the matter. Not at all. This is *Christian Doctrine*. What the author fails to realize is this: *sin doesn't keep us from repenting.* An illusion sustained by God—which keeps us in sin—keeps us from repenting. When the illusion is lifted, repentance will follow automatically.

The truth will set you free. From what? From the illusion that causes sin. How telling it is that a simple five word statement about the nature of truth gives the lie to its two greatest enemies.

# 12

# Arminianism

IN THE PREFACE TO this book I wrote:

> Often Universalist apologists make their case as if Calvinists did
> not exist . . . That is something this book will seek to redress. Let
> me use another illustration. The author of a Universalist blog pens
> an essay in which he sets out to
>
> *"reveal a very important Biblical Truth . . . Knowing this truth
> will automatically lay to rest many myths and misconceptions . . .
> So what is this Truth? Simply this: That everything, absolutely ev-
> erything, always goes according to the will and the plan of God.
> Always!"*
>
> He then proceeds to quote dozens of verses that assert the
> absolute sovereignty of God over all things, including man's will.
> And he makes a compelling case. There's only one problem: The
> Calvinist *already* believes everything he says about God's sover-
> eignty. They just believe He *uses* that sovereignty differently. The
> Calvinist and the Universalist are doing different dances to the
> same music!

An Arminian might have the same reaction to my book as a Calvinist
might have toward those Universalist authors. They might say: Okay, so
you believe that God is the Universal Father. So do I. That doesn't mean all
men will be saved. We are doing different dances to the same music!

Fair enough. I have argued as if all that's required to prove Universalism is to disprove Calvinism. In point of fact, that's exactly what I *do*
believe. On this matter I agree with Thomas Thayer who wrote:

"This places the subject in its true position; and the old Calvinistic ground . . . is the only ground on which the doctrine of endless woe can make any show of defense. If a single soul be damned, it is because it was created for this end, foreseen and foreordained. It was the original thought and plan of God in creating it, and not because he has made a mistake; not because the soul is anything different from what he expected; not because its faculties have been so perverted, to his great grief, that the design of its creation is defeated. This is the only consistent and logical ground for those who assert the omnipotence and omniscience of God."[1]

Calvinism is indeed the only consistent and logical ground for defending eternal torment. But then again, men are not always consistent and logical, are they? The fact is that Arminianism does exist and Calvinists themselves often employ Arminian precepts when it suits them to do so. For instance, they will argue that we are not sinners because we sin; we sin because we are sinners. That's classic Calvinism. We act according to our natures. But then when the subject turns to Adam and Eve, they will turn around and say the exact opposite. Our sin did not flow from our nature; it contradicted it! That's classic Arminianism. This Chameleon-like quality is a staple of Calvinism. Basically, they will employ any argument that's convenient to defend their theological system. And so any argument against Arminianism actually is also an argument against Calvinism; hence it suits my purposes to include such arguments in this book. I have enumerated at great length the logical inconsistencies of Calvinism; I will attempt something similar with regard to Arminianism. Specifically, I will attempt to refute the Arminian position with an appeal to five things:

1. Romans 9:19

2. Human nature

3. The nature of freedom

4. The relationship between law and grace

5. Experience

1. Thayer, *Theology of Universalism*, 87.

## 1. Romans 9:19

We begin with a quote from Romans 9:13–18. We begin here because the question raised in this section, combined with the answer given in verse 19, ought to be enough to settle the question. The passage reads:

> "As it is written, Jacob have I loved, but Esau have I hated. What shall we say then? Is there unrighteousness with God? God forbid. For he saith to Moses, I will have mercy on whom I will have mercy, and I will have compassion on whom I will have compassion. So then it is not of him that willeth, nor of him that runneth, but of God that sheweth mercy. For the scripture sayeth unto Pharoah, Even for this same purpose have I raised thee up, that I might shew my power in thee, and that my name might be declared throughout the earth. Therefore hath he mercy on whom he will have mercy, and who he will he hardeneth."

Verse 11 already stated that this decision had been made *before* either man had been born in order to make it perfectly clear that man's works and will had no bearing on it. Now verse 19: "Thou wilt say then unto me, Why doth he yet find fault? For who resisted his will?"

Consider the implications of such a statement. If God had chosen Jacob over Esau because He had foreseen that Jacob would *accept* Him and Esau wouldn't, then the objection would have never arisen in the first place. It would simply be a matter of fairness. God is rewarding Jacob's faith and punishing Esau's faithlessness. Who could possibly object to that? If an objection did arise to such a decision, it would certainly have taken a different form than the one anticipated by Paul. But look at the words: " . . . *Why* doth he yet find fault?" Remember the old Bud commercial—Why ask why? Well, it's an apt question if Arminianism is true. Why ask why? Why, if God is simply responding to one man's goodness and to the other man's wickedness, is anyone asking *why*? Stephen E. Jones writes:

> "In the time of the New Testament, there were three main religious parties in Judea, and each differed in their teaching on predestination. The *Essenes* believed totally in predestination . . . Opposed to them were the *Sadducees* . . . Josephus tells us that the Sadducees believed in total free will . . . The *Pharisees*, on the other hand, stood in the middle . . . All of these form a backdrop for Paul's teachings and were quite well known to Paul. Thus, he is not likely to be ambiguous in his words . . . In this context, he says in the ninth chapter of Romans [goes on to quote 9–13] . . . So we see that

Paul takes the case of Jacob and Esau as prime examples of God's Election, showing that God chose them *before* either of them had done good or evil. Keep in mind these are Paul's *examples* to prove the doctrine; they are not exceptions to the rule . . ."[2]

The simple fact of the matter is that Romans 9:13–19 clearly refutes the claims of Arminianism.

## 2. Human Nature

It seems to me that anyone who insists on the primacy of the human will in determining one's eternal destiny must choose between one of two alternatives. They are:

1. We sin in accordance with our nature

2. We sin against our nature

Both choices present obvious problems. If number one is the case, then Adam sinned because he was created a sinner. If number two is true, then Adam's sin did not reflect his true nature. This raises the obvious question: Why would he sin if it was not in his nature to do so? Richard Oerton writes:

"Cardinal Basil Hume was, by all accounts, a very good and kindly man. When he was archbishop of Westminster he used to walk at night through the streets around the Cathedral. Suppose that on one of these walks he came upon an old lady lying on the pavement, obviously ill or injured, barely conscious but still alive. The street is deserted. There is no one to see him. Is he going to reassure her, try to make her comfortable, get help . . . or is he going to kick her savagely in the head and go on his way smiling? We feel so sure of the answer that we think the question stupid and insulting: surely, if he took the second course, it could only be because of some sudden, catastrophic, pathological event in his brain. But suppose there was no such event and that he did take that course nonetheless, and suppose that his crime were discovered. Imagine a newspaper headline: *"I don't know what came over me," says the Archbishop, "It must have been free will"* . . . This is the sort of effect which, every day, we expect free will to achieve."[3]

2. Jones et al., *Creation's Jubilee*, ch 11.
3. Oerton et al., The Nonsense of Free Will ch 14.

Let's suppose that the traditional idea that Adam sinned against his nature is correct. What are the implications of such a thing? Does this increase his guilt or reduce it? How would this play out in any court of law? Does any criminal get a harsher sentence because his crime did *not* reflect his true nature? Would a judge ever issue the following verdict: "I believe this heinous action of the defendant did not in fact reflect his true character. It was in no way in keeping with who I believe this man to be. I am therefore going to add an additional five years to his term."

Of course such a thing is ridiculous. We all know the justice system does not work that way, nor do we think it should. And yet, it seems, we do think that God's justice system works that way, and we defend it.

But even if we allow for a kind of magical free will that can at once reflect one's character and still rise above it, we do not solve the problem. In fact, we make it worse. Let's say, for the sake of argument, that we do have this kind of free will. We are not merely the sum total of physical processes. There's a spirit, a soul, a ghost in the machine somewhere that's directing matters. Does this change anything?

Not really. This means we have two factors involved in human decision making: the ghost in the machine and all of the external stimuli that affects the person's decision. The ghost is the constant and the stimuli are the variables. If this is true, then a certain conclusion follows from it: A person should not be expected to always respond the same way to the same stimuli. If he did, then the the stimuli, not the "ghost" is the only relevant factor. This means that if a person found himself confronted by the same exact set of stimuli twice, he should be able to respond differently the second time. The "ghost" (the constant) should be able to process the stimuli (the variables) and respond to them in a different way. Is this likely? Let's consider the case of Adam. What if Adam had been given a do-over?

Imagine the following scenario: We are back in the early days of man. Adam, at 40 years of age, begins to suffer from a severe case of amnesia. Bit by bit, piece by piece, all of his memories fade away. Remarkably, all of the taint of sin also falls away. His desires return to their post-fall state, as does his physical constitution. Virtually everything about him is the same as it was before he ate the forbidden fruit. Even his pre-fall memories return, although not his post-fall memories. As the past recedes into nothingness, he finds himself wandering into a garden. Shortly after, the Lord puts him into a deep sleep and creates a women out of his rib. Shortly after that he and the women—named Eve—are forbidden to eat of the fruit of the tree of the knowledge of good and evil. Now, what do you suppose is going to happen?

I believe we all know the answer to that question. He will eat the fruit, of course. The question is: Why? How can we know he will eat the fruit? Or even believe that it's likely? If Adam has free will, then how do we know what he will do? This certainty is not possible under the prevailing understanding of original sin. This understanding is that Adam was created perfect—or nearly so. He was placed in an environment in which sin was extremely unlikely. It should be likely, therefore, that this do-over would yield a different result. The "ghost" (the constant) should be expected to respond to the stimuli (the variable) in a different way. And yet we know that he wouldn't. How can this be?

This might sound like a clever rehashing of an old argument, namely this: If any of us had been in Adam's shoes, we would have done the same. If all men would have done the same as he did, then does this not amount to an acknowledgment that sin springs from man's nature, and therefore he ought to be forgiven for it? But there is an answer to this argument that doesn't apply to our do-over illustration. Yes, all men, if they had been in Adam's shoes, would have sinned. Man, by nature, is a sinner. But this sin-nature came *from* the fact that Adam sinned, and we were all in principle *in* Adam. Therefore the fact that all men *would* have sinned had they been in Adam's shoes does not absolve them; this very fact arises from the fact that we all *did* sin. In Adam. We don't sin because we are sinners; we're sinners because we sinned. It comes from a nature that *we* created.

But this argument does not work in the do-over example. In this case Adam is no longer tainted by any sin. You can't say he would sin again due to a nature that he himself corrupted. He is "good" again. He's Perfect Adam again. Now, if he has free will of a *relevant* kind, he will almost certainly not sin again. The odds are all against it. How, then, do we know he will? I submit that it is the very fact that a do-over must yield the same results that accounts for the fact that God did not—and could not—give Adam a do-over.

But let's suppose for a moment that I have spoken presumptuously. Let's suppose that maybe—just maybe—a do-over might have yielded different results. Does this prove the primacy of the will and hence justify the traditional position on this subject? To the contrary, it actually works *against* the traditional view. If Adam might have responded differently on different occasions, now you have a situation where God, for all practical purposes, just caught Adam on a bad day. If he had been given another shot, he probably would not have sinned. Indeed he probably would not have sinned once in a thousand times. God just happened to catch him on the one day that he happened to respond to God's command in a way that destroyed his entire race. On this model, Adam could never have really been guilty *or* innocent. In order to establish guilt, there had to be a fixity to Adam's decision; it had to reflect his character. And so too with innocence. If he were to be innocent, than it would have to reflect that same fixity. Which means simply this—the guilt could only come from Adam's nature; the innocence from Christ's nature. Which sounds an awful lot like this: "Therefore as by the offense of one judgment there came upon all men to condemnation; even so by the righteousness of the one the free gift came upon all men unto justification of life" (Romans 5:18).

What God had in view for Adam is a different kind of second chance. A *real* second chance. This means to be given the same options *combined* with knowledge of the consequences of having made the wrong choice the first time. Put Adam back in the garden *minus* that knowledge, and he is not being given a second chance at all. You are simply guaranteeing a replay of the original outcome. But again, this should not be so if Adam had true freedom the first time. Why would an additional factor be needed in order to constitute a second chance? What is this to say except that were a *free* Adam given a million chances he would have failed every time? And what is that to say except that Adam, although free in a technical sense, was not free in a relevant sense? Is this fact not incontestable proof that Adam *had to sin*, even as the bible insists, when it says that flesh and blood cannot inherit the kingdom of God (1 Cor. 15:50)? And that the natural man cannot obey the law (Romans 8:8)? And that man was made subject to vanity (Romans 8:20)? And that we are free only to the extent that Christ makes us free (John 8:36)? And that everything acts in accordance with its nature (Matthew 12:33)? We've heard the evangelists say it a thousand times: We're not sinners because we sin; we sin because we're sinners, only to turn around and say that we *became* sinners because we sinned. What a contradiction of both logic and scripture!

The fact is that another chance would not have yielded a different result *unless there was an additional added factor*. That factor is *experience* with the results of the decision. It was, in effect, impossible to give Adam a second chance *as he was originally*. Adam could never have a second chance *as Adam. Christ* is Adam's second chance. Adam had to fail, as evidenced by the following scriptures:

> "The first man Adam was made a living soul; the last Adam was made a quickening spirit." (1 Cor. 15:45)

> "Now this I say, brethren, that flesh and blood cannot inherit the kingdom of God; neither doth corruption inherit incorruption. (1 Cor. 15:50)

> "It is sown in corruption; it is raised in incorruption." (1 Cor. 15: 42)

> "That which is born of the flesh is flesh; and that which is born of the Spirit is spirit." (John 3:6)

> "They that are in the flesh cannot please God." (Romans 8:8)

> "Either make the tree good, and his fruit good; or else make the tree corrupt, and his fruit corrupt: for the tree is known by its fruit." (Matthew 12:33)

Christ, on the other hand, cannot fail.

> "Whomsoever is born of God . . . cannot sin" (1 John 3:9)

> "Either make the tree good, and his fruit good; or else make the tree corrupt, and his fruit corrupt: for the tree is known by its fruit." (Matthew 12:33)

> "As in Adam all die, so in Christ shall all be made alive." (1 Cor. 15:22)

Adam never got a *first chance.* Our destiny was never meant to be found in Adam; it was meant to be found in Christ. Where is the evidence that Adam ever enjoyed an intimate relationship with Christ? Or that God ever loved him as one loves a child? There is not the slightest hint of such a relationship. God does not truly love a person until they are saved—until they are *in Christ.* And contrary to every thing the Christian religious system says, this was true of Adam as well. God did not love Adam (mankind) and never will until he is *in Christ.*

## 3. The Nature of Freedom

John 8:36 says "If the Son therefore shall make you free, ye shall be free indeed." The bible never talks about free will. The bible knows only of two things: freedom in Christ and slavery to sin. A person is free, according to the bible, precisely to the extent that He is being *subjected to Christ*. That is why we are not born free, but rather slaves to sin and concluded in disobedience (Romans 11:32). This principle is illustrated by two verses:

> "No man can come to me, except the Father . . . draw him" (Jn 6:44)
>
> "All the Father giveth me shall come to me; and he who comes I will in no way cast out." (John 6:37)

There's no middle ground; those not drawn cannot come and those drawn cannot refuse. Repentance is merely a matter of seeing things as they really are. Anyone who sees God as He truly is *will* repent. 1 John 3:2 states: ". . . we shall be like him; *for we* shall see him *as he is*." Notice what this verse is saying and what it's not saying. It is not saying "we shall be like him *and* we shall see him as he is." It is saying we shall be like Him *for we* shall see Him as He is. In other words, a clear vision of God *will produce repentance*. 2 Cor. 3:17–18 says: "Now the Lord is the Spirit; and where the Spirit of the Lord is, there is liberty. But we all, with unveiled face, beholding as in a mirror the glory of the Lord, are being transformed into the same image from glory to glory, just as by the Spirit of the Lord." The darker the mirror, the less of Christ you will see in it, and the more of yourself. The word is the mirror. The clearer it gets, the clearer Christ gets. What does a mirror reflect? Our own image, of course. The bible was meant to reflect to us our own image. At *first*. The clearer it becomes, however, the less of our own image we see and the more of Christ's. Why? Because we are being transformed into that image as we see deeper into the word. The clearer our vision, the more we will see of Christ in that mirror. The more clearly we see Him, the more we are transformed into His image. When we see Him perfectly, we *must* become like Him. When the man *in* the mirror is Christ, the man *staring* in the mirror must be Christ-like. This is a simple matter of cause and effect, and free will does not enter into the equation.

The mistake people make is to imagine that repentance is a matter of God wrenching us out of the natural order of things into a new order, when in fact it is the current condition that is unnatural. God must take heroic measures not to get us out of it, but to *keep us in it*. He must blind us from the truth *lest we repent* (Mark 4:12–15).

The myth of eternal torment has made us believe the very opposite. It was *so hard* for Christ to redeem us; after all, had to suffer eternal torment to do it. We have been lead to believe that God, who created us in Himself and for Himself (Col. 1:16), had to strain Himself beyond measure in order to reclaim a few of us. Nonsense. The truth is that He's shutting eyes and closing ears and hardening hearts to keep men from repenting (Mark 4:12). 2 Timothy 2:25–26 says " . . . in meekness instructing those opposing—if perhaps God may grant them repentance to an acknowledging of the truth, and they may awake out of the devil's snare . . ." Awake! We are asleep; to bring about repentance God need only nudge us awake. Remember, we were created *in* Christ and *for* Christ. He *is* our life, and we are heading back *to* Him ( Col. 1:16, Rom. 11:36). He is our source and our inevitable destination. For now, God is delaying what will inevitably happen when we see him *as he is*. We have not yet seen him that way. George MacDonald writes:

> ". . . the notion that a creature born imperfect, nay, born with im-
> pulses to evil not of his own generating, and which he could not
> help having, a creature to whom the *true face of God was never
> presented, and by whom it never could have been seen* (emphasis
> mine), should be thus condemned [to everlasting torment] is as
> loathsome a lie against God as could find place in a heart too un-
> developed to understand what justice is, and too low to look up
> into the face of Jesus. It never in truth, found place in any heart,
> though in many a pettifogging brain."[4]

## 4. Law and Grace

I believe a simple observation of the relationship of law and grace is all that's needed to dispel the claims of Arminianism. It's a tenet of Christianity that Christ came to release man from the bond of the law. How, exactly, does this happen according to an Arminian understanding? What is the scenario? It is something like this: You are under the law. As such, you stand condemned, for all have transgressed the law. But there's good news. Christ came to save sinners. He paid your sin debt on the cross. He loves you and wants you to be saved. If you accept Him you will be free from the condemnation of the law.

Now, here's where the tricky part comes in. Notice the word *if.* This two letter word, it seems to me, creates an insurmountable obstacle to the Arminian position. It means, to some extent at least, that the ball is still in our court. If we accept Him, we will be saved. If we don't, we will not.

4. George MacDonald as quoted in Thomas Talbott's *The Inescapable Love of God* 12.

Now, the bible is clear that "accepting" Christ means obedience. "If we say we love him and obey not then we lie . . ." (1 Jn 1:6). We cannot, therefore, remove all—or any—demands of the law by this *if*. Accepting Christ does not release us from the demands of the law. Indeed the command to "accept" Him—and therefore to obey Him—is made even more urgent, and the penalty for refusal is even greater. How, then, are we better off under Christ than under the law? Let's break it down.

> You are under the law.
>
> Christ will free you from the law and its penalties.
>
> *If* you obey Him.
>
> And if you fail the penalty will be even worse.

It's hard to see how this system makes Christ anything other than another law, and a worse one at that. This is not hard to understand. We know that the law worketh only wrath (Rom. 4:15). Then Christ comes, saying "Obey me or the penalty will be even worse." Again, the question arises: How are we better off? Isn't Christ *increasing* the power of the law by his threat? Isn't His ministry an even *greater* ministry of condemnation than that of the law? The usual answer to this charge is something like this: *The penalty is greater now because grace is greater. Christ gives us a greater ability to obey the law; therefore the penalty is also greater.* This mindset is evident in the way evangelicals preach these days. They make it sound like rejecting Christ's grace is akin to holding back the sea. They would have us believe that one can only get to hell by a truly heroic resistance of God's grace against all the odds.

But this will will not do. It completely ignores the *biblical* relationship between grace and law. Law increases sin. Threats increase sin. It doesn't matter whose name is affixed to the law—Jehovah or Christ. Why would it? Especially if Christ *increases* the penalties involved. If God increases the threats of the law proportionally to the dispensing of grace, then the two cancel each other out. As grace makes us stronger, the law makes us weaker, leaving us right back where we started. In other words, if the *penalty* of the law increases *proportionally* with grace, then how does grace help us keep the law? The bible says, "where sin abounded grace much more abounded" (Romans 5:20). But if the penalties increase proportionally with grace given, then the truth is that "where grace abounds, the law abounds all the more."

But if this is true, then how can a man be saved? He can only be saved according to a Calvinist understanding of law and grace. It is not a matter of God exerting His grace upon our wills, hoping to bend them to his own, and failing more often than He succeeds. That's nonsense. God doesn't fight with us to get us saved. He "has mercy on whom He will have mercy" (Rom. 9:15). He draws irresistibly, exactly as the Calvinist says. The Universalist, however, believes that He will draw all men, whereas the Calvinist limits it to a few.

## 5. Experience

The following is an excerpt of an article that appeared in a magazine.

> "Tommy McHugh was 51 years old when blood clots in his brain destroyed his old self—and caused a new personality to emerge. He went from an ex-con and heroin addict one day to a sensitive artist the next. This transformation debunked an old myth: The core self is not immutable . . . The two blood clots in the brain of Tommy McHugh hit the 51 year old like a ton of bricks . . . McHugh awoke from a coma as a new man . . . Prior to the emergency surgery, McHugh was a ruthless thug. At fourteen he dropped out of school and ended up in prison for various violent crimes. He also became a heroin addict. Since he awoke from his coma, however, McHugh has been writing poetry and painting pictures like mad. His craving for a heroin fix has vanished, and violence disgusts him. His works of art have hung in galleries from London to New York. But how can someone simply lose his personality, and a new one come to light? Is it possible in each of us lies a second dormant personality, an alter ego that lurks beneath the first one? And if so, what needs to happen to trigger the process to bring forth this hidden identity? . . . In McHugh's case, the blood clots damaged just enough of his brain's inhibiting connections to allow his previously suppressed creativity—his concealed personality—to come through . . ."[5]

I close this chapter by posing to the Arminians one simple question, upon which the answer will either prove or disprove the validity of their theological system. The question is this: Is God more powerful than a stroke? It's a fact of modern life that science is constantly discovering new

5. ID magazine, *Can a Single Moment of Your Life Reprogram Your Whole Personality?* (*Englewood Cliffs*, NJ: Heinrich Bauer Publishing Co. 2012) p 60.

chemical causes for effects previously ascribed solely to the human will. Indeed science has discovered so many chemical, behavioral, cultural, and environmental causes for our behavior that the idea of free will itself has been called into question. And yet we insist that the sum total of this massive array of impersonal causes, which clearly shape a man's personality, are, in the final end, more able to transform a man either for good or bad, then the intelligent designer and cause of both the man and all causes affecting him. How can we believe that documented cases of transformation wrought by proximate causes can exceed the transformations possible by the root cause of all causes and all effects? Such a thing is clearly impossible. It is impossible from a philosophical perspective, a chemical perspective, a biological perspective, and a psychological perspective. But for those who insist it is possible from a scriptural perspective, I would simply refer them to the following thirty five verses.

> 2 Chronicles 18:19–22 "And the LORD said, "Who will persuade Ahab king of Israel to go up, that he may fall at Ramoth Gilead?' So one spoke in this manner, and another in that manner. Then a spirit came forward and stood up before the LORD and said, 'I will persuade him.' The LORD said to him, 'In what way?' So he said, 'I will go out and be a lying spirit in the mouth of all his prophets.' And the LORD said, 'You shall persuade him and also prevail; go out and do so. Therefore look! The LORD has put a lying spirit in the mouth of these prophets of yours, and the Lord has declared disaster against you."

> Amos 3:6 "Shall there be evil in a city, and the Lord hath not done it?"

> Isaiah 45:7 "I form the light, and create darkness: I make peace, and create evil: I the Lord do all these things."

> Isaiah 13:11 "And I have appointed on the world evil, And on the wicked their iniquity, And have caused to cease the excellency of the proud, And the excellency of the terrible I make low."

> Job 14:5 "Since [man's] days are determined, the number of his months is with You; You have appointed his limits, so that he cannot pass."

> Psalm 139:16 "Your eyes saw my substance, being yet unformed. And in Your book they were all written, the days fashioned for me, when as yet there were none of them."

> Proverbs 20:24 "A man's steps are of the LORD; how then can a man understand his own way?"

Jeremiah 10:23 "O LORD, I know the way of man is not in himself; it is not in man who walks to direct his own steps."

Job 23:13,14 "But He is unique, and who can make Him change? And whatever His soul desires, that He does. For He performs what is appointed for me, and many such things are with Him."

Romans 11:36 "For of Him and through Him and to Him are all things . . ."

Acts 15:18 "Known to God from eternity are all His works."

Job 42:2 "I know that you can do everything, and that no purpose of Yours can be withheld from You."

Isaiah 46:10 "Declaring the end from the beginning, and from ancient times things that are not yet done, saying, My counsel shall stand, and I will do all My pleasure."

Daniel 4:32,35 " . . . the Most High rules in the kingdom of men, and gives it to whomever He chooses. All the inhabitants of the earth are reputed as nothing; He does according to His will in the army of heaven and among the inhabitants of the earth. No one can restrain His hand . . ."

Acts 4:28 "They gathered to do everything that you, by your power and will, had already decided would take place."

Ephesians 1:11 "In Him also we have obtained an inheritance, being predestined according to the purpose of Him who works all things according to the counsel of His will."

Jeremiah 18:6 "O house of Israel, can I not do with you as this potter?" says the LORD. "Look, as the clay is in the potter's hand, so are you in My hand, O house of Israel."

Proverbs 21:1 "The king's heart is in the hand of the LORD, like the rivers of water; He turns it wherever He wishes."

Isaiah 63:17 "O LORD, why have you made us stray from Your ways, and hardened our heart from Your fear?"

Proverbs 16:1 "The preparations of the heart belong to man, but the answer of the tongue is from the LORD."

Acts 22:14 "The God of our fathers has chosen you that you should know His will, and see the Just One, and hear the voice of His mouth."

Romans 8:29-30 "For whom He foreknew, He also predestined to be conformed to the image of His Son, that He might be the firstborn among many brethren. Moreover whom He predestined, these He also called; whom He called, these He also justified; and whom He justified, these He also glorified."

John 1:12–13 "But as many as received Him, to them He gave the right to become children of God, to those who believe in His name: who were born, not of blood, nor of the will of the flesh, nor of the will of man, but of God."

John 6:44 "No one can come to Me unless the Father who sent Me draws him: and I will raise him up at the last day."

John 15:16 "You did not choose Me, but I chose you and appointed you . . ."

Ephesians 1:4–5 "He chose us in Him before the foundation of the world, that we should be holy and without blame before Him in love, having predestined us to adoption as sons by Jesus Christ to Himself, according to the pleasure of His good will."

Ephesians 2:10 "For we are His workmanship, created for Christ Jesus for good works, which God prepared beforehand that we should walk in them."

Philippians 2:13 "For it is God who works in you both to will and to do for His good pleasure."

2 Thessalonians 2:13 "But we are bound to give thanks to God always for you, brethren beloved by the Lord, because God from the beginning chose you for salvation through sanctification by the Spirit and belief in the truth."

2 Timothy 1:9 "[God] has saved us with a holy calling, not according to our works, but according to His own purpose and grace which was given to us in Christ Jesus before time began."

1 Peter 2:19 "But you are a chosen generation, a royal priesthood. A holy nation, His own special people, that you may proclaim the praises of Him who called you out of darkness into His marvelous light."

Psalm 58:3 "The wicked are estranged from the womb; they go astray as soon as they are born, speaking lies."

Isaiah 48:8 "Surely you did not hear, surely you did not know; Surely from long ago your ear was not opened. For I knew that you would deal very treacherously, and were called a transgressor from the womb."

1 Peter 2:8 "They stumble, being disobedient to the word, to which they also were appointed."

Revelation 13:8 "All who dwell on the earth will worship him [the beast] whose names have not been written in the Book of Life of the Lamb slain from the foundation of the world."

# 13

## The Danger of Relying on Mystery

FINALLY, I WOULD LIKE to close this book by cautioning the Calvinist about relying too much on mystery. They would do well to remember that God can do things with mystery that we can't even imagine. Indeed it may be God's mysterious will to populate hell with only Calvinists, and He can do it by employing nothing more than the very logic the Calvinists use to defend His right to damn the rest of us. I will demonstrate how.

Five point Calvinist Harold Camping hosted a radio call in program called the Open Forum. He received many calls from friend and foe alike. Some called to argue, some to agree, some to just say *keep up the good work*. But one caller stood out from the rest. He called a lot. A real lot. In fact, he called all the time. Sometimes he would even disguise his voice so as not to violate Camping's rule that listeners restrict themselves to no more than one call per month. He seemed particularly aggrieved over Camping's teachings that God had reprobated most of humanity to hell and that there was nothing anyone could do about it. He would try desperately to pin Camping down on the issue, searching for inconsistencies, and even quoting Camping's own words back to him in an effort to refute him. A typical exchange might begin with: "On march 8th you said—and I quote . . ." And then he would proceed to make his case, often throwing in more quotes. Camping, of course, held fast to his position, defending it with the usual verses, and the exchanges never amounted to much. And yet the man called back again and again and again to argue his case.

But it didn't take a great deal of psychological acumen to see that there was more at work here than just a difference of opinion. If the caller truly had as much contempt for Camping's opinions as his remarks indicated, he would have not kept calling back. The fact that he did surely meant something. Why did he *care* if Camping agreed with him or not? Obviously, Camping held a certain sway over him. And this, it seemed to me, was the real problem. He hated Camping's teachings, but *feared* that they were true. And so he kept calling in a desperate attempt to prove that they weren't. He seemed to be pleading with Camping to change his mind or, at the very least, to modify his position somewhat. He seemed to be pleading with Camping to stop preaching such an awful God. More importantly, perhaps, he seemed to be pleading with him to stop *siding* with such a God. The unspoken subtext that reverberated through his incessant, impassioned calls was that Camping, by agreeing with God on this matter, was somehow complicit in the harsh position that God was taking. He seemed to be arguing not so much with Camping as he was with *God*. And finally, after years of taking the man's calls, Camping called him on this very thing, telling the man: *You're problem's not with me; it's with God.*

Actually, I believe his problem was with God *and* Camping. Allow me to explain. The Calvinist believes that God has divided the world into the elect and the non-elect, the first to serve as vessels of His love, the second as vessels of His wrath. His purpose in eternally tormenting the non-elect is to demonstrate His justice and his mercy *to the elect*. In this respect, it might be argued—and probably *felt* by that caller—that the elect, by their acquiescence to such a plan, are *encouraging* God to enforce it. And I believe they have a point.

Let's break this down. Suppose you are God. You are seated in your temple devising your plan to divide the world into the elect and the non-elect. You envision the elect praising you throughout eternity for saving them. The praise is made even more heartfelt by the fact that they are permitted—yes, even obliged—to watch from heaven as their non-elect former friends and relatives are tormented in hell. This very aspect of the equation gives an accent to the salvation of the elect, demonstrates the supererogatory nature of your mercy, and, of course, gives you greater glory. The torment of the non-elect *enhances the quality of the worship you receive from the elect.* They worship you more fervently than they would have had everyone been saved.

Now, let this marinate for a moment. Consider the implications and your own complicity in this scheme. And then ask yourself: But what if God knew that no-one whose brother He damned would ever worship him at all? And what if He knew that his glory *could not* be appreciated by the elect unless He also elected their brothers (and sisters)? Would He have had to modify His plan? If so, then are the elect complicit in the eternal torment of the non-elect by their cowardly acquiescence to a plan whose justice, to the very best of their ability, they cannot now appreciate?

Yes, one might answer, but this assumes that I have the ability to change God's plans, which, of course, I do not. True enough. But the fact remains that God predicated his plan on the fact that He could receive *willful* worship from creatures whose brothers and sisters He would torture forever. How does that let you off the hook? How does it make your actions any more noble? You are merely shifting the blame from man to God, which, as any Calvinist knows, simply does not wash. The justice of hell itself is predicated on the idea that God, as the *primary* cause of sin, still has the right to hold man—the secondary cause—responsible for his sins. And thus if the aforementioned action is cowardly and ignoble, then this fact—according to *Calvinist* theology—is not mitigated by the fact that God pre-ordained it. In fact, according to *Calvinist theology*, God would be entirely just in sending Calvinists to hell for *being Calvinists*. Hiding your cowardice behind the skirt of God's sovereignty just won't cut it.

In closing, I would just caution the Calvinist that the bible says it is an unpardonable sin to attribute to God the works of the devil (Mark 3:22–30, Mt. 12:31–32), and that they seem dangerously close to committing this sin. Moreover, if they do find themselves in hell one day, they may also find themselves on the wrong end of their own logic. Indeed they may find themselves having the following conversation.

God: "Depart from Me; I never knew you."

Calvinist: "But why, Lord?"

God: "For slandering My holy name by saying that I would ever damn anyone."

Calvinist: "But you are! You're damning me!"

God: "And rightly so; I damn those who deny My love. I damn Calvinists and only Calvinists. This way I affirms My love and My justice at the same time. You must admit, it's an ingenious way of demonstrating My sovereignty and the supererogatory nature of My mercy."

Calvinist: "But this whole thing is a contradiction!"

God: "I prefer *mystery*. Now, away with you!"

# Bibliography

Allin, Thomas., et al. *Christ Triumphant.* Canyon County, CA: Concordant Publishing Concern, (no year given). Online http://www.tentmaker.org/books/ChristTriumphant

Armstrong, Karen. *A Short History of Myth.* New York: Cannongate Books Ltd, 2005.

Ballou, Hosea., et al Randolph: (VER.), 1805 Online http://www.biblicaluniversalism.org/PDF/A.TreatiseOn.Atonement.pdf

Beauchemin, Gerry. *Hope Beyond Hell.* Olmito: Malista Press, 2010.

Bell, Rob. *Love Wins.* New York: Harper Collins Publisher, 2011.

Burnfield, David, *Patristic Universalism: An Alternative to the Traditional View of Divine Judgment.* Universal-Publishers, 2013 (e-book).

Camping, Harold. *To God Be The Glory!* Oakland, CA: Family Stations, Inc., 2008.

Camping, Harold. *God's Magnificent Salvation Plan,* Oakland, CA: Family Stations, Inc., 1999.

Camping, Harold. *First Principles of Bible Study:The Bible is its own Interpreter,* San Jose, CA: Good Message Foundation, 2001.

Camping, Harold. *The Perfect Harmony of the Numbers of the Hebrew Kings.* Oakland, CA: Family Stations, Inc. 2008.

Cottington, Gary. "The Mother of All Truths." No pages. Online http://hell-fact-or-fable.com/2010/04/the-mother-of-all-truths

Cottington, Gary. "The Lucifer Myth." No pages. Online http://hell-fact-or-fable.com/2010/04/the-lucifer-myth-2/

Cottington, Gary. "Genesis Reloaded." No pages. Online http://hell-fact-or-fable.com/2010/04/the-tree-of-the-knowledge-of-good-and-evil

Eby, Preston. "Eternity." No pages. Online http://www.kingdombiblestudies.org/savior/SOW1htm

Eby, Preston. "The Serpent." No pages. Online http://www.kingdombiblestudies.org/serpent/Serpent.htm

Eby, Preston. "The Two Hands of God." No pages. Online http://www.kingdombiblestudies.org/2hands/2hands1.htm

Eby, Preston. "The Law of Circularity." No pages. Online http://www.godfire.net/eby/circularity.html

Eby, Preston. "Echoes From Eden." No pages. Online http://www.godfire.net/eby/echoes/eby-echoes_from_eden_part39.htm

Eby, Preston. "The Restitution of all Things." No pages. Online http://www.godfire.net/eby/restitution.html

## Bibliography

Eckerty, Ken. "Does Man Have Free Will?" No pages. Online http://savior-of-all.com/freewill.html

Farar, Canon et al., *Mercy and Judgment*. London: The Macmillan Company, 1904. Online http://www.tentmaker.org/books/mercyandjudgment_ch1.html

Fudge, Edward. *The Fire That Consumes: A Biblical and Historical Study of the Doctrine of Final Punishment*. Lincoln: Verdant Publications, 2001.

Guthrie, C. Shirley. *Christian Doctrine: Revised Edition*. Louisville: Westminster/John Knox Press, 1994

Heintzman, J. David et al., *Man Became A Living Soul*. No pages. Online http://www.harvestherald.com/mbls/chapter_one.htm

Israel, Jacob. "Garden of Eden Revisited." No pages. Online http://jacobisrael.com/2010/01/02/garden-of-eden-revealed/

Jones, E. Stephen et al., *Creation's Jubilee*. Fridley, MN: God's Kingdom Ministries, 1995. No pages. Online http://www.gods-kingdom-ministries.net/teachings/books/creations-jubilee

Knoch, E. Adolph., et al. *All in All*. Dallas, TX: Concordant Publishing Concern

Oerton, Richard, *The Nonsense of Free Will*. Matador, 2012. (e-book)

Pridgeon, H. Charles. *Is Hell Eternal? Or Will God's Plan Fail?* Pittsburgh: The Evangelization Society of the Pittsburgh Bible Institute, 1920.

Rauser, Randal. "Why Calvinists Should be Universalists or Armenians." No pages. Online http://randalrauser.com/2011/11/why-calvinists-should-be-universalists-or-Armenians/

Smith, L. Ray. "Twelve God-Given Truths to Understand His Word." No pages. Online http://bibletruths.com/twelve.htm

Strahan J. and Meeker M. "Whose in Charge?" No pages. Online http://www.restoreallthings.org/styled/styled-8/styled-14/

Talbott, Thomas. *The Inescapable Love of God*. USA: Universal Publishers/u PUBLISH. com, 1999.

Thayer, B. Thomas. *Theology of Universalism: Being an Exposition of Its Doctrines and Teachings*. Boston: Tomkins and Company, 1863.

Tolle, Eckhart. *The Power of Now*. Canada: New World Library, 1994.

ID magazine, *Can a Single Moment of Your Life Reprogram Your Whole Personality?* Englewood Cliffs, NJ: Heinrich Bauer Publishing Co., 2012.

Manufactured by Amazon.ca
Bolton, ON

28957992R00109